Contemporary Approaches to Moral Education

Analyzing Alternative Theories

Contemporary Approaches to Moral Education

Analyzing Alternative Theories

BARRY CHAZAN
The Hebrew University of Jerusalem

TEACHERS COLLEGE PRESS

Teachers College, Columbia University
New York and London

Published by Teachers College Press, 1234 Amsterdam Avenue,
New York, N.Y. 10027

Library of Congress Cataloging in Publication Data

Chazan, Barry I.
   Contemporary approaches to moral education.

   Bibliography: p.
   Includes index.
   1. Moral education.   2. Education — Philosophy.
I. Title.
LC268.C45   1985   370.11′4   84-26785

ISBN 0-8077-2765-2

Manufactured in the United States of America

90 89 88 87   2 3 4 5 6

For Shai and Tali

Happy the father, mother of these!
From "On the Portrait of Two Beautiful Young People"
by Gerard Manley Hopkins

CONTENTS

PREFACE

TWENTY-FIVE YEARS AGO, the introduction to a volume on moral education would begin with a reservation about venturing into relatively uncharted waters; today the starting point for such an introduction is an apology for yet another book on this subject. The past two decades have been the occasion of a remarkable explosion in reflection, experiment, and programming related to moral education—which has generated a plethora of articles, books, symposia, instructional materials, professional organizations, and professional appointments in that area.[1] The lament of Hare and others in the 1950s and 1960s about the neglect of moral education in philosophic and educational circles is now outdated.

As we enter the waning years of the twentieth century, we can point to the emergence of a significant number of theories and programs of moral education that are studied in universities and/or are implemented in schools and other educational settings. These theories have periodically been described and summarized; however, there has not been a systematic, comparative analysis of the philosophical and educational underpinnings of these various theories. That is the task of this volume.

In 1973, Jonas Soltis and I edited a reader, *Moral Education*, which attempted to introduce some order into the emerging discussion of moral education by relating it to key concepts of moral philosophy.[2] This volume builds on those key concepts and utilizes them as a prism for the analysis and comparison of several major theories of moral education. In addition, key concepts and categories that have emerged in the practice of moral education are employed in this analysis.

I have had to be selective in my choice of theories, and hence this volume does not claim to include all contemporary theories and certainly not all the current programs of moral education. Generally, the focus is on theories that reflect an elaborate and comprehensive model of morality and moral education (e.g., Durkheim, Wilson, Kohlberg, Dewey), that present a detailed practical program of moral education (e.g., values clarification), or that come to reject the very enterprise of moral education (the anti-moral educationists). Thus, while I cannot hope to be exhaustive in my choice of theories, I have selected major twentieth-century exemplars of schools of moral education to raise most of the key issues.

ix

My discussion and comparisons are based on the analysis of texts in which the approaches have been presented. In most cases, these texts constitute carefully developed theoretical presentations which, accordingly, invite a patient textual analysis. Some of the theories are presented in practical or programmatic documents, rather than in precisely developed philosophic treatises. Hence, it has been necessary to utilize different styles of analysis, depending on the texts in question. Generally, this volume is most profitably read in conjunction with the primary texts, rather than instead of them. (Abbreviated examples of several texts appear in the reader, *Moral Education*; others are available in sources cited in the respective chapters.)

Indeed, my main concern is not to summarize views; nor do I wish to deprive readers of the great excitement of directly confronting texts themselves. My aim is rather to analyze, categorize, and compare.

My overall goal in this volume is more modest (but I trust no less important) than "good old" moralizing and moral philosophizing; it is to help educators to reflect more carefully and precisely on the great issues involved in the activity of moral education. I trust that such an enterprise too may be considered as amongst the most moral of human activities.

ACKNOWLEDGMENTS

ALONG WITH THE IMPRESSIONS of places and events, many teachers and students, knowingly or not, have influenced my thinking about moral education over the years; while I cannot record all the individual names, their contributions are significant and are appreciated. Jonas Soltis and Israel Scheffler have guided my academic work in the area of philosophy of education for two decades; they have been masterful teachers and colleagues. Professor Scheffler read the first four chapters of this book and made helpful comments. I have had the privilege of an ongoing discussion of many of the issues raised in the book with Michael Rosenak; he is a friend and the quintessential teacher. My discussions with Mordechai Nissan and Joseph Reimer about moral development and education, and specifically about cognitive-developmental moral education, have been most enlightening. I thank Professor Nissan for reading Chapter 5. My extended family has been a source of warmth, learning, and fun for many years and in many places, and I thank them all. I should particularly like to note the contributions of Blanche Kirschenblum and Mildred Kirschenblum; they are unique people.

Nomi has reflected, shared, and worried with me about the issues I have herein dealt with, and her very being teaches about the subject of this volume; Nomi, I am grateful. This book is dedicated to my children Shai and Tali. They are in Hopkins' words, two beautiful people who have made me happy and, I hope, a bit more moral.

Contemporary Approaches to Moral Education

Analyzing Alternative Theories

Chapter 1

THE ISSUES
OF MORAL EDUCATION

WHILE MORAL EDUCATION would appear to be the most practical of educational ventures, encompassing the everyday realities of school and classroom life, it actually involves some of the most basic and profound issues of human existence. Some dimensions of moral education reflect questions that have traditionally preoccupied moral philosophy; other aspects relate to themes in the domain of educational philosophy; and certainly, some of the issues of moral education are directly linked to the actual lives of schools and classrooms. Hence, the analysis of approaches to moral education must encompass three conceptual categories: the philosophic, the educational, and the practical. This book analyzes several prominent twentieth-century schools of moral education via all three categories, with major emphasis on the first two. In this chapter, I shall delineate nine parameters (five from moral philosophy, two from educational philosophy, and two from educational practice), which shall serve as the criteria for the analysis and comparison of our twentieth-century schools.

ISSUES IN MORAL PHILOSOPHY AS RELATED TO
THE PRACTICE OF MORAL EDUCATION

The sphere of philosophy known as 'moral philosophy' or 'ethics' deals with a broad range of topics that generally revolve around the elucidation of such concepts as 'good', 'right', 'ought', 'duty', and 'moral'.[1] It is impossible to delineate one exclusive set of assumptions or conclusions held by moral philosophers throughout the centuries; instead, we find a rich collection of alternative definitions and theories. At the same time, there do seem to be some common issues or questions about the 'moral sphere' that have concerned most moral philosophers; that is, there is some semblance of an agenda of topics related to the sphere that is shared by the many philosophers who have reflected on the moral sphere. These agenda items (or "topics of moral philosophy") also constitute important foci of reflection for any practical program of education concerned with 'morality'. Hence,

1

we have isolated five types of issues frequently dealt with by moral philosophers that shall serve as categories to be used in our analysis of schools of moral education: (1) the social and the individual, (2) moral principles, (3) reason in ethics, (4) content and form, and (5) action. It should be noted that these are not the only issues that have been dealt with by moral philosophers nor is this the only way to categorize them. Instead, these five foci may be regarded as the parameters of one representative, analytic prism.

The Social and the Individual

Is 'morality' essentially a group phenomenon or an individual experience?[2] Does the term morality refer to a collection of norms, values, and behaviors of a specific group (e.g., the 'morality' of the middle class), or does it refer to an individual's free and considered choice of one behavior rather than another? What is the source of 'morality': group norms or individual conscience? These questions reflect some of the major issues of discussion and disagreement among classical and contemporary moral philosophers. Some thinkers have regarded 'morality' as a code or ethos rooted in a collective authority, in which case 'the moral way' would imply behavior in accordance with the norms of the collective. An alternative philosophic tradition has argued that 'morality' refers to a modal experience of the individual, a form of personal confrontation that each individual must undergo. In this case, to be 'moral' implies the ability to confront and resolve certain categoric types of problems, rather than adherence to an external set of norms. Both of these conceptions conceive of the question of the individual or social nature of morality within the context of the broader philosophic discussion of the meaning of human nature.

The issue of the social and/or individual nature of morality is clearly a matter of great concern for educational practice. If morality is essentially social, then moral education has the responsibility to transmit and inculcate the collective moral code; if morality relates to individual reflection and choice, then moral education's function would be oriented to the development of qualities indispensible for individual reflection and choice. Hence, this issue of moral philosophy has far-reaching implications for the practice of moral education.

Moral Principles

A second important issue of moral philosophy focuses on the role and nature of principles in moral philosophy.[3] The moral sphere is in part characterized by the existence of statements denoted as 'moral principles', which seem to play some sort of role in the moral behavior ultimately chosen by an individual. Philosophers have, consequently, been concerned with clarifying the meaning and role of such statements in the moral sphere. This concern encompasses the following sorts of questions: What kind of statement is a moral principle? Is it factual, emotive, imperative, evocative, normative? Are moral principles generalizable statements applicable across time and place, or are they local and temporal statements that are determined by specific contexts? What moral principles are the most worthwhile: justice, truth, liberty, pleasure, the good of the group, honesty?[4]

The issue of 'moral principles' is surely a central question for the practice of moral education. Much of what goes on in schools is related to words, sentences, and statements, and the meaning and functioning of moral principles is obviously relevant in such a context. Hence, the most practical questions of moral education are very much dependent on the elucidation of the linguistic status and functioning of moral sentences, the universal or relative nature of moral principles, and the validity of alternative contents implicit in various moral standards.[5]

Reason in Ethics

Is there any connection between reason and ethics?[6] This topic has been one of the perennial concerns of moral philosophers and has resulted in the emergence of some major alternative theories of moral philosophy.[7] There are several issues which characterize the discussions: (1) Does reasoning have any place in morality? (2) If it does, what is the exact way in which moral reasoning functions? (3) Is moral reasoning unique or is it similar to other forms of reasoning? (4) What is the relationship between moral reasoning and moral action? (5) What is the relationship between moral reasoning and habit? (6) What is the relationship between moral reasoning and passion? (7) Is morality dependent on the ability to reason?

The consideration of these questions parallels some of the most basic issues of the nature of education, that is, the role of reason, habit, passion, and norm in the educational sphere. Traditionally, of course, education and reason (or at least intellect) have been regarded as appropriate bedfellows; the moral philosopher asks about the connection between reason, morality, and education. Surely, no program of moral education can become operational until it responds to that query.

Content or Form

Some moral philosophers, particularly of late, have asked whether 'morality' is ultimately a specific *content* or *normative stance*, or rather a *process* or *procedure* that is defined by certain technical characteristics?[8] According to the former approach, 'morality' refers to specific ideologies or normative philosophies (e.g., concern for others, concern for self, love of homeland, the will of God), which are translatable into detailed and specific norms. According to the latter approach, 'morality' refers to procedural characteristics that imply how we should confront a moral problem, without necessitating or predetermining a specific outcome. The latter approach often compares 'morality' to such activities as driving, swimming, or studying history, in which we learn certain skills that can then be applied to a variety of situations or settings (once you know how to drive you should be able to do so in a Ford, Pontiac, or MG, and/or to travel to the barbershop, the bar, the church, or the cinema as you desire; the skill does not predetermine where you will go).

This topic has particularly preoccupied recent approaches to moral education (especially those influenced by early- and mid-twentieth century moral philosophy). Some philosophers and educators have argued that moral education should teach particular moral contents and world views; that is, moral education should be about the transmission of moral ideologies. Others have argued that, given the heterogeneity of modern life and the nature of morality, moral education should teach the *process* of morality; that is, moral education should be about the development in children of the ability to operationalize the general process of confronting moral issues. These are two widely divergent conceptions of moral education that emerge from the philosophic debate on form and content in the moral sphere.

Action

Deeds and action have been regarded as central dimensions of the moral sphere by moral philosophers throughout the centuries. Indeed, we might well hazard the claim that this sphere reflects greater consensus among moral philosophers than any other; to be 'moral' in some way is assumed to imply the performance of certain deeds and actions. At the same time, philosophers have debated several issues concerning the relationship of morality and action. One important question has to do with the relationship between 'knowing' and 'doing' in the moral sphere — what the educational philosopher William Frankena has called the dialectic between MEX (moral education X) and MEY (moral education Y).[9] Does increased knowledge necessarily lead to increased moral deeds, or not? Indeed, there are apparently many examples in contemporary education (often in affluent, suburban school systems) of quality, intellectual education that does not seem to be accompanied by parallel moral deeds. Thus, while philosophers may agree that morality implies action, educators want to know how such action is stimulated.

A second question related to the action sphere that has preoccupied moral philosophers is the relationship between *intention* and action. Is moral action a question of the performance of certain deeds via whatever means are effective (e.g., punishment, information, candy, or love) or must it somehow flow from a conscious deliberate choice — a consummate act of will by an individual? Can there be genuine moral action that does not flow from moral intention? This issue too is a primary educational issue, for it will have profound implications for the means, techniques, and measures used in education. Indeed, the resolution of this issue of moral philosophy is indispensable for both short-range practical pedagogic issues and long-range educational directions.

THE INTERRELATION BETWEEN THESE FIVE ISSUES

These five issues constitute some of the major concerns of moral philosophers throughout the ages. While there is no definitive consensus about them, it is possible to delineate some clearly distinguishable categories of responses. Moreover, specific responses to each of these questions sometimes coalesce into clearly delineated, organic moral philosophies. Indeed, it may well be argued that an organic moral philosophy is one that deals with these five (and other) philosophic categories in an internally logical and consistent fashion. The more internally consistent a theory is, the more convincing it might be as the basis for a program of moral education. Hence, while our main concern in this volume is to examine the ways in which these five philosophic issues (along with the four issues to be next discussed) are treated in our respective schools of moral education, we shall periodically examine the degree of organic interrelation and integration (or contradiction) among responses to each of these questions *within* a specific approach.

ISSUES IN THE PHILOSOPHY OF EDUCATION RELATED TO THE PRACTICE OF MORAL EDUCATION

A growing literature in the philosophy of education in recent decades has focused on basic issues in moral philosophy that relate to educational contexts. Thus, philosophers of education have dealt with the relationship between moral knowledge and moral action in the educational sphere;[10] the interrelationship of reason and habit in moral education;[11] the role of moral principles in education;[12] socialization and autonomy in moral education.[13] Many of these topics are rooted in the analysis of some of the basic issues of moral philosophy that we have just enumerated. However, two topics that have preoccupied contemporary philosophers of education are worthy of analysis as unique new categories: (1) a conception of 'the morally educated person' and (2) 'indoctrination' and moral education.

A Conception of the Morally Educated Person

Who is the 'educated person'? This is a question with which philosophers of education have continuously wrestled; the resolution of this question has been regarded as critical for any attempt to build a theory or practice of education.[14] Similarly, philosophers of moral education have attempted to develop criteria for the 'morally educated person'. Is such a person one who performs good works? Is he/she[15] a person who *thinks and acts* in certain ways? Must he/she be committed to a specific set of moral principles? Is the morally educated person one dimensional or multidimensional?

Certainly, an image of the ideal student we would like to "produce" is of great importance for the educator. Such an ideal — even if unattainable — provides a direction and framework for the practical educational activity. Hence, it is no wonder that educational philosophers have increasingly devoted time to this issue.

'Indoctrination' and Moral Education

The issue of 'indoctrination' has become a prominent theme of recent moral educational philosophy.[16] The following questions preoccupy those who are concerned with the issue of 'indoctrination' and moral education: (1) What are the distinguishing criteria of 'indoctrination'? (2) Are moral, religious, and political education the paradigm examples of 'indoctrination'? (3) What are the differences between 'indoctrination' and 'education'? (4) Is education possible without 'indoctrination'?

The unifying factor of most discussions of 'indoctrination' is the negative connotation usually ascribed to the term. Most analysts begin from the assumption that 'indoctrination' is an undesirable activity, and the thrust of their effort is to isolate those qualities that represent the negative nature of the enterprise.

The attempt to distinguish between 'good' education and 'mis-' or 'undesirable' education (which is ultimately what people want to imply by use of the term 'indoctrination') is, of course, of great importance for educational practice, since it has specific implications for what will or will not be done in the classroom. Indeed, the detailed analysis of 'indoctrination' in the context of moral philosophy ultimately presupposes the general discussion of what we believe 'education' should or should not be. Hence, it is no wonder that educators have been concerned with the elucidation of this topic.

NONPHILOSOPHIC ISSUES IN PROGRAMS OF MORAL EDUCATION

We have suggested that practical programs of moral education are, in some way, related to and informed by the elucidation of larger issues (or prior questions) of moral philosophy and the philosophy of moral education. At the same time, there are a host of issues related to the practice of moral education that are not inherently philosophic, but that are, nevertheless, of great importance for the analysis of schools of education. We shall, therefore, include the following two practical educational issues in our comparative analysis.

The Role of the Teacher

What does it mean to be a 'teacher of moral education'? Who should or should not engage in this activity? Must the teacher of moral education have special skills, knowledge, abilities? Can the average teacher implement complicated theories of moral education? How do we train teachers for such an enterprise? How does the already over-burdened teacher introduce yet another subject into his/her busy day? These are but a few of the practical questions that teachers, teachers of teachers, administrators, and lay leaders must confront when discussing the topic of moral education. As the architects of many creative educational programs and curriculum projects have painfully learned, many great ideas and programs have been rendered ineffective because they did not take into consideration the myriad issues related to the teacher. Hence, we shall examine the treatment of the teacher in the various schools of moral education that we shall study in order to arrive at a complete sense of the theory.

Pedagogy, Methods, Procedure, and Materials

The philosopher sits in his office and thinks about the grand problems of morality and education while the teacher searches for a story, or mimeographs worksheets for this morning's class. Education ultimately is realized in materials, activities, and programs that are reasonably accessible, interesting to students, and offer some promise of success. The analysis of moral education must also deal with the nature of the educational materials proposed; how the materials will be used by teachers; the relation of the topic of moral education to other subjects in the curriculum; and the costs in dollars and cents. Thus, we shall conclude the analysis of each school of moral education by examining its particular conception of and suggestions for the practical pedagogic domain.

SUMMARY

In this chapter, we have delineated nine issues from three spheres (moral philosophy, philosophy of moral education, and the practice of moral education), which together constitute the prism through which we shall examine the respective schools of moral education:

Moral Philosophy
1. The social and the individual
2. Principles
3. Reason in ethics
4. Content and form
5. Action

Philosophy of Moral Education
6. The conception of the morally educated person
7. Indoctrination and moral education

The Practice of Moral Education
8. The role of the teacher
9. Pedagogy (methods, procedures, materials)

Our task in this volume is to utilize these nine parameters as the grid through which we shall examine contemporary schools of moral education. The use of this multidimensional prism will enable us to understand the many meanings of the term 'moral education' in twentieth-century educational thought.

Chapter 2

EMILE DURKHEIM: MORAL EDUCATION AS MORAL SOCIALIZATION

OUR DISCUSSION OF CONTEMPORARY APPROACHES to moral education begins by returning to the turn of the century and the writings of the French sociologist, Emile Durkheim. Durkheim may well be considered to be the father of modern moral education. While he is a neglected and/or maligned figure in current discussions of moral education, he, in fact, established the conceptual realm of discourse that continues to characterize any contemporary analysis of moral education. Durkheim's comprehensive treatment of moral education encompasses the issues, problems, and concepts that concern theorists and practitioners of moral education today. Moreover, there is a sense in which many of the contemporary approaches to moral education are responses to and reactions against a Durkheimian approach; hence, he is the appropriate starting point for our discussion.

INDIVIDUAL VERSUS SOCIAL

Durkheim is usually considered to be the paradigmatic spokesman of a social conception of morality.

> Moral goals are those the object of which is: society. . . . The domain of the moral begins where the domain of the social begins.[1]

> Morality begins with membership of a group; it is not related to an act which has individual interests [alone].[2]

> No one will deny that no act has ever been regarded as moral which is oriented exclusively to the preservation of the individual.[3]

> It is not a simple juxtaposition of individuals who bring an intrinsic morality with them, but rather man is a moral being only because he lives in society, since morality consists in being with a group and varying with this solidarity. Let all social life disappear, and moral life will disappear with it, since it would no longer have any objective.[4]

> Without society, morality has no object, duty, no roots.[5]

Morality is, then, according to Durkheim, an inherently social phenomenon and fact, comprised of a body of social rules and activities. It is created by societies and aimed at societies. The social character of morality is an indispensable minimal necessity in defining the phenomenon. Moreover, morality is a real phenomenon in itself, not reducible to or explainable by more basic or primitive individualist drives, forces or instincts. (Hence, Durkheim rejects ethical egoism as a viable moral theory because of its postulation of the interests of the individual as the basic moral factor.[6])

This definitive stance on the social origins of morality as an objective fact is the source of much of the discontent of current approaches to moral education, which are uncomfortable with a notion of morality as a body of social norms and conventions that are arbitrarily imposed on the young.[7] For Durkheim, however, the issue is clear: "Man is man, in fact, only because he lives in society.[8]

Thus, morality is not, for Durkheim, a question of the lonely individual's quest for the moral way outside of the moral conventions and dictates of society. Morality outside of the moral conventions and dictates of society does not exist, and the quest of the lonely individual (so popular in contemporary moral literature) would not be a moral issue in Durkheim's system. Hence, the very distinction between individual and social morality, which is the starting point of some contemporary approaches, is rejected from the outset by Durkheim.[9]

However, Durkheim's treatment of this subject is made complicated and sophisticated by his notion of the "two spheres" or the dual nature of man.[10] The essence of this argument is that there is an individual and personal being of man as opposed to the social or impersonal being.[11] In his paper, "The Dualism of Human Nature and Its Social Conditions," Durkheim characterizes the distinction as between sensations and sensory tendencies versus conceptual thought and moral activity,[12] or the egoistic and the personal versus universalized, impersonal conceptual thought. The one being is composed of all the mental states that apply only to "ourselves" and to the events of our personal lives, whereas the social being is a system of ideas, sentiments, and practices that express in us the group or different groups of which we are part. It is only in the second being that morality can be regarded as existing, and, indeed, "to constitute this being in each of us is the end of education."[13]

Durkheim's writings present somewhat different explanations of the dynamics of the interaction between those two selves. Usually, Durkheim writes of the social being as a creative and sustaining source for the individual; it essentially creates his existence as a moral being. "Society is the benevolent and protecting power, the nourishing mother from which we gain the whole of our moral and intellectual substance and toward whom our wills turn in a spirit of love and gratitude."[14]

Thus, the social being is neither a problem nor a burden for the individual; on the contrary, it is a life-giving resource. Instead, it is the separation from institutions and supportive social groups that is the dysfunctional state and that is one of the causes of egoistic or anomic suicide.[15] The emergence of the social self is the desired state and in it lie the origins of order, meaning, and morality. It is in unity with and membership in institutions and society rather than in separation and isolation from them that the true origins of men's creativity are to be found.[16]

The second explanation of the interrelationship between the individual and social self in Durkheim (a position that according to Lukes and Wallwork surfaces toward the end of Durkheim's life) focuses more on the antagonism between the two selves.[17] In a passage remarkably reminiscent of Freud's *Civilization and Its Discontents*, Durkheim says:

> In brief, this duality corresponds to the double existence that we lead concurrently: the one purely individual and rooted in our organism, the other social and nothing but an extension of society. The origin of the antagonism that we have described is evident from the very nature of the elements involved in it. . . . Society has its own nature, and, consequently, its requirements are quite different from those of our values as individuals. . . . Therefore, society cannot be formed or maintained without our being required to make perpetual and costly sacrifices. . . . Therefore, since the role of the social being in our single selves will grow even more important as history moves ahead, it is wholly improbable that there will ever be an era in which man is required to resist himself to a lesser degree, an era in which he can live a life that is easier and less full of tension. To the contrary, all evidence compels us to expect our effort in the struggle between the two beings within us to increase with the growth of civilization.[18]

This position assumes that there will be an (increasing) tension between the "I" (the personal self) and the "me" (the social self) that will be resolved only by the realization and dominance of the social self. The sense of tension suggested by this passage becomes a major motif of subsequent educational thought, although the latter usually sees the resolution in the emergence of the "I" at the expense of society.

One of the problems that surfaces in a social notion of morality such as Durkheim's is the role of rebellion and nonconformity. Specifically, how does Durkheim account for such recognized moral figures as Jesus or

Socrates who seemed, in fact, to thwart and reject the norms and conventions of the societies in which they lived?

Durkheim deals with this issue in the discussion that follows his paper on "The Determination of Moral Facts,"[19] where he, in fact, turns Socrates and Jesus into examples of the very type of moral person he is advocating. Jesus and Socrates are frequently presented as examples of individuals not bound by conventional morality, but true to their own reflections and considerations and ultimately obeying a higher ideal. Durkheim does not accept the notion of a "higher" ideal in the sense of one eternal moral ideal binding for all. However, he does regard Jesus and Socrates as moral exemplars in the sense that they were rebels *in the name of society*; that is, theirs was a rebellion of the true collective against the conventional collective. They were not individualistic rebels against society, but rather they were the authentic spokesmen of the genuine social morality of their times ("Socrates expresses more clearly than his judges, the morality suited to his time"[20]). They were not angry young men nor was their rebellion antisocial; rather, they were true social beings fighting for a better and truer vision of society.

Durkheim uses this example to argue that social morality is not necessarily equivalent to conventional morality or to what the majority of the people do, and morality cannot always be determined by majority rule or consensus. Indeed, there are moments when the most moral of actions will appear to be the most antisocial or nonconformist.

We should not, however, let this illusion of individualism color the truly social nature of moral existence. As Durkheim points out, "The objection has been made to this conception that it [society] subjugates the mind to the prevailing moral opinion. . . . The society that morality bids us desire is not the society as it *appears* to itself, but the society as it is really becoming."[21]

In emphasizing the importance of Durkheim to contemporary thought, Ernest Wallwork suggests that Durkheim's notion of the "social self" has become a dominant motif of contemporary social science, political science, philosophy, theology, and education:

> The concept of the "social self," which Durkheim helped introduce into modern thought, has largely supplanted, in the course of the twentieth century, the "rational self" of the Enlightenment and the "economic self" of the early nineteenth century . . . "sociological man" now clearly vies with Freud's "psychological man" and Kierkegaard's "existential self" as the "dominant moral type of contemporary Western culture."[22]

Ironically, the main dynamic of much of contemporary moral educational theory would seem to be just the opposite of Durkheim's "social self." Much of contemporary moral education would seem to constitute a reaction against Durkheim and an attempt to replace the "social self" with some of the supposedly supplanted models, for example, the "rational self," "psychological man," or the "existential self." This reaction is one of the themes that we shall examine in this book.

MORAL PRINCIPLES

There are three questions central to a discussion of Durkheim's approach to moral principles and moral education: (1) What are 'moral principles'?[23] (2) Is there a body of overriding moral principles that reflect *a priori* moral values or ideals? (3) What role do moral principles play in human life and moral education?[24]

Basic to Durkheim's discussion of the entire topic of moral principles is his distinction between moral facts ("les faits moraux") and moral ideals. There are in the world, Durkheim argues, phenomena called 'moral facts';[25] they constitute a category of natural "things" and, hence, can be studied in an objective, scientific fashion—that is, in terms of a science of moral facts whose task is to determine the distinctive features of what is moral.[26]

Moral facts have several characteristics. First, as already noted, they are social in nature and, in fact, are subcategories of the phenomenon of 'social facts'.[27] The social nature of moral facts is not derivative; it is inherent in and integral to the definition of 'morality' and 'moral facts'.[28]

Second, moral facts are rules of conduct:

> [Morality] is not a system of abstract truths which can be derived from some fundamental notions, posited or self-evident. . . . It belongs to the realm of life, not to speculation. It is a set of rules of conduct, of practical imperatives which have grown up historically under the influence of specific social necessities.[29]

> All morality appears to us a system of rules of conduct.[30]

A moral fact is a type of statement that contains a prescription or directive as to specific actions that we must perform. Such statements have inherent in them the power of authority; they are statements that imply obligation, duty, and sanction:

> Moral rules are invested with a special authority by virtue of which they are obeyed simply because they command.[31]

Third, moral facts include the notion of desirability and goodness:

> Obligation or duty only expresses one aspect abstracted from morality. A certain degree of desirability is another characteristic no less important than the first.[32]

Thus, morality is also about actions that have some worth or appeal to the performer.

Durkheim's notion of moral facts becomes clearer when seen in terms of the attempt to respond to and reconcile a Kantian notion of morality as implying obligation and duty with the utilitarian motif of morality as an empirically rooted practice, reflective of human needs and desires.[33] While Durkheim was unable to accept the *a priori* metaphysical assumptions of Kant, he did accept his emphasis on morality as authority. Similarly, while he was unable to accept what he regarded as the overly individualistic and hedonistic nature of utilitarianism, he did accept its emphasis on morality as an empirical phenomenon reflective of human realities and desires. Thus, the facts (and their more formal organization as systems of morality) imply, non-*a priori*, empirically and socially rooted duties and obligations, which reflect desirable and worthy actions.

Moral ideals are a second category of moral statements dealt with by Durkheim.[34] Moral ideals refer to a body of standards that a society sets for its members. These standards are embodied in the institutions, traditions, and precepts of the society, and they constitute what a society wishes to transmit to its young.[35] In what he regarded as a major reversal of classical theories of morality, Durkheim argued that moral ideals are derivative from moral facts, rather than moral actions being deduced from an *a priori* body of abstract moral ideals. Such ideals not *a priori*, universal, or nonempirical in nature, but rather are generalized statements derived from concrete realities. For Durkheim, moral ideals are not beyond experience, but lie within the empirically verifiable: "These ideals are simply the ideas in terms of which society sees itself."[36] Such ideals are the soul of a society and function as powerful, dynamic collective forces.

Thus, moral ideals for Durkheim constitute the elevation and sanctification of social-moral facts. At one point in his discussion of moral ideals, Durkheim resorts to an uncharacteristically metaphysical style in distinguishing between 'moeurs' as "that morality which men actually observe throughout history and which is vested with the authority of tradition"[37] and 'morale' as "ideal morality situated in a region above the realm of human action."[38]

Several points now become clear about Durkheim's notion of moral principles. First, there is no one body of moral principles in the sense of an *a priori* universalizable set of statements that determine the moral life of all humanity. Second, the notion of moral principles is not rooted in individualistic instincts, but rather in society and in man's social nature, which are the true first principles of human existence. Third, morality is a system of specific rules of conduct reflective of the moral realities of specific societies, and these rules are given authority and sanction by virtue of their importance to that society.

Durkheim's notion of 'moral principles' as herein elucidated combines several disparate elements, which has often led to popular overemphasis on one element rather than another. Thus, sometimes Durkheim is depicted as exclusively concerned with moral norms and obligatory action, whereas, in fact, he was probably more concerned — particularly in his later writings — with moral ideals.[39] At other times, Durkheim has been depicted as being radically relativist in his moral stance and, hence, essentially committed to a self-determined, nonobligatory ethic,[40] whereas his system is, in fact, radically nonindividualistic and heavily committed to a notion of obligation and duty as imposed from outside the individual. Finally, Durkheim is often accused of being concerned with the promulgation of a conventional, conformist moral order and moral education, whereas his approach emphasizes the role of reason, especially inductive reasoning, and some notion of autonomy in the moral domain; (see our prior discussion of Jesus and Socrates according to Durkheim and the next section on "Reason in Ethics").

The reason for these various (mis-) interpretations lies in a fact noted earlier, that is, the underlying attempt of Durkheim's work to react to some prominent classical ethical theories and to reconstruct them in a radically new synthesis (what Wallwork calls the two basic philosophic perspectives of Durkheim's entire scholarship: "neo-naturalism" and "relational social realism").[41] Durkheim was attempting to create a new (inter-) marriage, and the respective families of the bride and groom often had eyes only for their particular child under the marital canopy.

Finally, we can turn to our third question: What role do moral principles play in human life and in moral education according to Durkheim? Moral principles, in the sense we have just discussed them, that is, as a set of rules or acts that predetermine conduct, are the essential subject and content of moral education. Moral education should not be about the teaching of a body of universal moral principles, or the teaching of processes of moral reasoning (per se), or the development of the ability to express moral stances or sentiments. Rather, it is aimed at morally socializing the individual to act in certain ways consistent with the norms and ideals of his/her society.

At the same time, since moral principles according to Durkheim are grounded in fact and are susceptible to scientific observation, they should not be taught in an exclusively rote or impository fashion. In a much neglected passage in *Moral Education*, Durkheim says that "to teach morality is neither to preach nor to indoctrinate; it is to explain."[42] Moral principles should function as directives and guides for moral life, which can and should be explained and explicated to children as the process of moral education. They constitute the heart of moral education, and they should be taught in a way that makes them obligatory actions, but at the same time ones that are reasonable and understandable. Moral principles are dynamic, reasonable social facts that are the creative force of meaningful moral life, and they should be transmitted accordingly.

REASON IN ETHICS

Durkheim's position on the place of reason in ethics reflects his broader commitment to what he considered an "uncompromising rationalism," that is, a belief that there is nothing in reality that is beyond the scope of human reason:

> The sole [label] that we accept is that of *rationalist*. Indeed, our chief aim is to extend scientific rationalism to human behavior by showing that, considered in the past, it is reducible to relations of cause and effect — relations that a no less rational operation can then transform into rules of action for the future. Our so-called positivism is nothing but a consequence of this rationalism.[43]

Consequently, both the procedure that Durkheim proposed for studying morality, and the skills that he regarded as crucial to being moral were related to the rational domain.

Durkheim's notion of rationalism is based on the assumption that there are facts and truths in the natural world that can be understood empirically. Society and social facts — of which morality is a part — are one important aspect of that natural world; hence, morality can be understood rationally. Indeed, the appropriate way to understand phenomena is to look at their manifestations in specific historical and social contexts, a methodology most clearly exemplified in Durkheim's analysis of the development of French education.[44] In developing this notion of rationalism, Durkheim flatly decries the assumption of the existence of *a priori* truths or thought processes;[45] instead, he regards reasoning itself as a socially conditioned process aimed at understanding social and other types of phenomena.

There are two implications from these assumptions vis à vis the relationship of reason to ethics. First, Durkheim argues that the only way to study or understand morality is rationally, that is, via "the science of moral facts."[46] The study of morality should not be pursued in the deductive style of the classical philosophers, who reflected on one (or more) basic moral truths and then imposed them on society; rather morality should be approached in an inductive fashion in which we first look at social moralities and then arrive at a notion of a particular morality.

However, this is not the only sense in which reason relates to morality. For Durkheim, reason also constitutes an aspect of *being* moral; that is, reason is not simply a meta-activity for scholars to use in understanding morality but also a first order skill of the individual trying to be moral.

Durkheim talks about three elements or components of being moral: (1) to respect discipline (discipline), (2) to be committed to a group (society), (3) to have knowledge of the reason for our conduct (autonomy).[47] The first two elements, of course, are those most prominently associated with Durkheim's theory of morality and moral education; however, in his writings on the subject the third component receives much attention and prominence.

Durkheim's third component refers to the ability of the person to come to understand and accept the legitimacy and good of the rules and norms that he performs. For Durkheim, to be free is to come to recognize intellectually and accept the nature and function of norms, rules, and patterns that the individual is already performing as a member of a particular society.

This, of course, is not a rational ethic in the Kantian sense, nor is it an autonomous ethic in the Kierkegaardian sense; Durkheim is not talking about autonomy in the sense of the individual confronting and acting upon major moral questions in solitude. Durkheim's moral person comes to understand and accept (in a calm and reasoned fashion) the moral answers that he/she is living in a particular society.

This conception of moral reasoning and moral autonomy is spelled out in educational terms in the second part of *Moral Education* and in "A Discussion on the Effectiveness of Moral Doctrines."[48] In *Moral Education*, Durkheim discusses practical, curricular questions related to the teaching of morality. In contradistinction to the usual emphasis on the centrality of aesthetics for moral education (because of the great idealistic, emotional, and inspirational value of literature, art, and music), Durkheim surprisingly focuses on science and history as the two important curricular areas for moral education. Aesthetics are more damaging than positive in moral education for "art makes us live in an imaginary environment; it detaches us from reality and from the concrete beings that comprise reality."[49] Science and history, on the other hand, lead to an understanding of and confrontation with reality; they are about "life in earnest," and morality is just that.[50] The role of teaching science and history should be to focus on collectives and completeness, to help students see larger social patterns and motifs, and to help them understand the complex dynamics of social life and morality.[51]

The point is further underscored in Durkheim's notion of the teaching of morality as encompassing the development of comprehension and explanation. We have already noted Durkheim's claim that the teaching of morality should be concerned with explanation, rather than with preaching or indoctrination. In "The Discussion on the Effectiveness of Moral Doctrines," Durkheim makes a distinction between "moral education" which is "the concern for the formation of habits and the awakening of sentiments and motivational representations" (i.e., aimed at action) and "the teaching of morality" (*enseignment*) which is the concern for bringing about comprehension and explanation (and which is not in itself a preparation for action).[52] The teaching of morality, according to Durkheim, should respond to the spirit of free inquiry of children:

> The child who leaves our schools must have some idea of the underlying reasons for the moral discipline he is asked to practice. . . . He must know not just what his duties are, but at least to a certain extent and varying according to age and level of culture, the wherefore of these duties. . . . We must therefore arm his intelligence with solid reasons which will stand up to the inevitable doubts and discussion.[53]

At the same time, it would be imprecise to read these usually neglected passages out of the larger Durkheim context; clearly, moral education for Durkheim is about moral socialization, and reasoning has a significant role, albeit in an *a posteriori* fashion. Children have to become moral agents in the social sense, and then they can and will understand the reason of their ways. Reason *is* a component of ethics, although not the only component. This point is perhaps best summed up in Durkheim's discussion with Belot on the role of rationality in ethics.[54] Belot defends the thesis of the centrality of rationality to morality, arguing that

> in social reality a moment always comes when individual consciences rebel against the collective imperatives and develop new imperatives. . . . Observation shows that there are isolated moments of conscience, of that spontaneous rational effort which tends to reorganize the system of rules and moral judgements."[55]

Durkheim admits that reflection "tends to become" an element of morality; however, he questions and ultimately contests Belot's claim that reflection is a necessary element of morality.

But I contest the fact that they [reflections and the social dimension] are both necessary. There is one which may be absent without morality ceasing to exist. . . . Even today we do not go so far as to say that for an act to be moral it must be reflective. . . . To be sure reflection raises and perfects morality, bu it is not the necessary condition of it.[56]

The often voiced claim that Durkheim's notion of morality neglects the individual and leaves little room for his reasoning and autonomy[57] has not been sensitive enough to what Durkheim actually wrote; at the same time, the contention that Durkheim is concerned with autonomy in ethics in the sense that some contemporary moral and/or educational philosophers talk about it is equally distortive. Durkheim's position on reason in ethics reflects his continuous attempt to synthesize a radically rational and scientific outlook (his neonaturalism) with a radically social perspective (his relational social realism).

FORM OR CONTENT

Is morality characterized by a certain style or approach or is it constituted by specific contents? Should moral education be about developing a process to deal with moral issues or should it be concerned with the transmission and development of moral *behaviors* and *actions*?

Morality is clearly, according to Durkheim, tied to specific contents, acts, rules, behaviors. It is a first-order phenomenon defined by a clearly and specifically defined body of rules.

[Morality] is not a system of abstract truth which can be derived from some fundamental notion, posited as self-evident. . . . It belongs to the realm of life, not to speculation. It is a set of rules of conduct, of practical imperatives which have grown up historically under the influence of specific social necessities.[58]

To be moral in this sense is not to employ a certain procedure, but rather to act in accord with a body of rules and norms.

At the same time, the picture of Durkheim's moral position which is emerging in this chapter suggests some reservations vis à vis an overly simplistic response to the issue in question. As indicated in the last section, Durkheim talks about three basic elements of morality: discipline, society, and autonomy. These elements are, according to Durkheim, "fundamental dispositions" as much as specific moral virtues. They are both substantive phenomena *and* procedures, skills, and abilities that can be applied to specific contexts (thus, discipline could mean obedience to the priests or the prophets, and society could refer to the gang or to someone's parents). Durkheim underscores the formal quality of teaching morality and/or of carrying out moral education when he states: "To influence the child morally is not to nurture in him a particular virtue, followed by another and still another; it is to develop and even to constitute completely, by appropriate methods, those general dispositions that, once created, adapt themselves readily to the particular circumstances of human life."[59] This notion of morality as described by Durkheim refers to duty, discipline, and society, without being accompanied by a specific bag of duties or list of social norms.

Indeed, a striking aspect of Durkheim's work on morality is the absence of sustained lists of specific moral rules or virtues that should be transmitted to children. His writings on morality and moral education are not primers of proper or desirable moral behavior, and even the more pedagogic sections of his writing do not contain exhaustive lists of desirable moral rules or virtues (something that theoretically could have been in his purview as a person responsible for the pedagogic department of his university). Part of the explanation for this feature, of course, lies in the fact that Durkheim saw his function as a professor in the academy who was concerned with helping students understand phenomena, rather than as a preacher or priest. Moreover, the very theory of morality that he was suggesting argues against any one definitive list of virtues that could be conclusively laid down for all groups. At the same time it would seem that there are elements within Durkheim's writings that suggest that morality was not exclusively a bag of virtue for him, but also included procedures and approaches for dealing with moral situations.

ACTION

Moral action is the central focus of the moral sphere according to Durkheim:

> Morality is a system of rules of conduct.[60]

> Morality consists of a system of rules of action that predetermine conduct . . . they state how we must act in given situations.[61]

Morality is directly expressed by the acts that we perform in the social arena. The concern for intention, motivation, and free will that characterizes much of the theological, psychological, and philosophic literature on morality are not basic to Durkheim's discussion of morality. Durkheim agrees that moral acts are neither blind nor arbitrary; they are performed in accordance with some system of rules of conduct and for a purpose, that is, for the sake of society. Thus, to be moral is not simply "to act," it is "to act for the sake of society."[62] In other words, moral action is linked to some justificatory system. However, such justification is not dependent on the individual's state of mind (or free will) prior to the act, but rather on a socially rooted ethic.

As noted, Durkheim's system has frequently been depicted as a socially imposed model of moral education that comes to subjugate the individual. In fact, it would be inaccurate to depict the action emphasis of Durkheim as programmed or behavioral. At the same time, there can be no denying that the "act" and the "deed" are central to Durkheim's system and significantly distinguish his system from the subsequent approaches to moral education that we shall discuss.

THE MORALLY EDUCATED PERSON

Our discussion of the morally educated person according to Durkheim will enable us to summarize several themes that have surfaced in our analysis. It should initially be noted that Durkheim's morally educated person would vary from society to society; that is, there is a sense in which there is no ideal, monolithic model of the morally educated person. Hence, the morally educated person is one who acts in accord with the moral climate and ideals of his/her particular society.

At the same time, there are certain apparently formal qualities of the morally educated person according to Durkheim; that is, there are dispositions and skills that schools can develop in children and that are necessary for them to function as moral agents in any society.

The three central abilities of the morally educated person are those previously mentioned: discipline (or duty), society, and autonomy.[63] These are qualities that Durkheim assumes to be inherent in the collective and individual life of the species and, therefore, able to be evoked and expanded in any child.[64] Moreover, these three qualities are not mutually inconsistent, and together they imply a healthy balance between excessive individualism and social authoritarianism. These three traits become main components of the curricular and cocurricular school program outlined in some detail by Durkheim in the second part of *Moral Education*.

The morally educated person is one who has learned (in school and elsewhere) to live in a way that reflects a sense and a practice of duty to a set of social ideals and norms. He/she is morally socialized in the sense that he/she acts consistently with ideals and practices valued by a society. Such duty and obligation should be accompanied by a sense of the goodness and value of such socialization. The morally educated person is one who has learned to act in certain ways and to be cognizant of and happy with his/her actions and values.

Durkheim was sensitive to attempts to overemphasize the potentially conformist nature of his moral system. Hence, as we have already noted, he utilizes the very figures presented as critiques of his system (i.e., Jesus and Socrates) as models of the desired moral person.[65]

Jesus and Socrates are moral exemplars for three reasons. First, both Jesus and Socrates are paradigms of the sense of duty and obligation; they were both willing to make the ultimate sacrifices out of a sense of duty to the right cause. Second, they were not private rebels against society; they were actually the true spokesmen of the genuine social morality of their times. Their rebellion was not antisocial; it was in the name of a better and truer vision of society. Finally, neither Jesus nor Socrates were programmed or conventional moral figures; rather, in the name of some loftier principle, they both were able to rise above human convention. They were people who came to realize, accept, and cherish the great ideals in whose name they spoke; they were, in that sense, free.

It should be emphasized that Durkheim's model takes seriously the notion of the morally *educated* person and the concept of *teaching* morality. Durkheim believes that the qualities of the moral person can and must be developed via intentional educative activities; they are not already developed internal traits in the individual. Thus, the teacher and the school can and should educate the person to be moral.

INDOCTRINATION

There is no detailed discussion of the concept of 'indoctrination' as such in Durkheim, although in various places he does deal with issues related to it.

One reading of Durkheim on this issue sees his notion of 'education' as close to the activity of indoctrination.

> Education is the influence exercised by adult generations on those that are not yet ready for social life. Its object is to arouse and to develop in the child a certain number of physical, intellectual and moral states which are demanded of him by both the political society as a whole and the special milieu for which he is specifically destined.[66]

This definition is frequently cited to support the position that Durkheim is ultimately interested in a top-down model of education, one that is concerned with the imposition of values and behaviors on children by adults, and one which, according to such arguments, constitutes 'indoctrination'.

Durkheim would reject the negative connotation implicit in attaching the term 'indoctrination' to his system. His position is not (as some apologists of indoctrination argue)[67] that indoctrination is a necessary evil;

that is, that it really is not good to impose facts, values, and behaviors on children, but we have no choice so we should do it as painlessly as possible. Durkheim has no such qualms or reservations; for him such imposition is not a necessary evil but a necessary good. The imposition of values is creation, not impingement. Not to impose would be evil and irresponsible, for it would be to deny the child the opportunity to be truly human.

At the same time, Durkheim does accompany his definition of education with some modifications aimed at preventing it from becoming an exaggerated model of imposition. First, he makes the distinction between 'moral education' and 'teaching morality' already noted.[68] The former, in fact, is reflective of his general definition of 'education'; the latter reflects his parallel concern for the analytic understanding of moral experience in social contexts. Second, in discussing the pedagogy of moral education, we have seen that Durkheim underscored the teaching of history and science (rather than aesthetics) because they: "help us better understand the human realm, and equip us with precise ideas, good intellectual habits which can help us in directing our behavior."[69] Aesthetic education, in fact, can lead to indoctrinating, because it removes us from reality and from prosaic reflection on what actually is. Third, Durkheim's notion of 'autonomy' would seem to constitute an antidote within his system to excessive imposition. The autonomous moral being is not imposed upon; he reflects, considers, accepts. He is not the passive object of the hypnotic metaphor of education presented in Durkheim's lecture "The Role of the State in Education";[70] he is an active, conscious, responding agent.

Hence, two opposite motifs in Durkheim combine to delineate a system that would seem to argue against its characterization as narrowly indoctrinary. Imposition of a certain sort at certain ages is regarded as positive, creative, and liberating (since without it a child could not become a full social being). However, there are elements built into Durkheim's approach to schooling that encourage and stimulate a child's inductive understanding of matters. Thus, for Durkheim moral socialization is a legitimate educational enterprise in that it helps the child find his/her place in a reasonable social order. *Not* to socialize morally is ultimately to indoctrinate because it implies letting fate, whim, or extraneous forces rather than reason and society determine morality.

THE TEACHER

Emile Durkheim spent a significant part of his professional career talking to and teaching prospective teachers, and his writings reflect a concern with several practical educational issues related to the role of the teacher and the nature of pedagogy and didactics.

It is clear that the teacher *has* to be central to Durkheim's system, because of the prior arguments of Durkheim's social philosophy, epistemology, ontology, and sociology. For Durkheim, learning is a social process whereby the young are influenced by the adult generation so as to give rise to a group of physical, intellectual, and moral states that are demanded by the social context. To know and to be moral is to be formed and influenced by society. The school, in fact, is the best agency in the modern age for this task, indeed, more important and appropriate for this function than the family: "Furthermore, contrary to the all too popular notion that moral education falls chiefly within the jurisdiction of the family, I judge that the task of the school in the moral development of the child can and should be of the greatest importance."[71] Clearly, then, the teacher as a key factor in the school, must occupy center stage in the moral socialization of children. Durkheim warned prospective teachers of the immense power that, by the nature of their positions, they would wield; indeed, rather than being discouraged by their impotence, Durkheim suggests that teachers should be frightened by their power.[72]

One of the central qualities needed to be an effective teacher, according to Durkheim, is *authority*: "Moral authority is the dominant quality of the educator."[73] The teacher must be a voice, symbol, and exemplar of discipline and sanction, both in order to typify for the child a key facet of the moral and social life and also to enable the teacher and the class to pursue their daily tasks with a semblance of order and efficiency. Such a function cannot always be effected happily — it frequently must be serious and somber. However, whether he is somber or not, an educator without authority cannot teach and will not develop in children the traits necessary for the moral life.

Such authority must be accompanied by a state of "faith and passion", that is, by the teacher's belief in the task and will to carry it out. The teacher must be a person of passionate commitments, much as the monks and other religious teachers of classical and medieval times were. ("The monk's life was . . . one which involved the active propagation of the faith. He was a preacher, a proselytizer, a missionary.")[74]

Another aspect of the teacher is the *totality* of his/her enterprise. Teaching is not about the transmission of isolated facts or tidbits; it is rather about a more organic, synthetic activity. Durkheim sees this emphasis as one of the great revolutionary changes effected by early Church education:

> In antiquity, whether Greek or Latin, the pupil received his instruction from different masters who were in no way connected with one another. Each of his teachers taught in his own house and in his own way. . . . There were no com-

mon motives or goals. Each teacher did his job on his own; one would teach reading, another the art of correct speaking, yet another would teach music and another the art of speaking as a learned person. But each of these activities was pursued separately. This is in dramatic contrast to what happened as soon as the first Christian schools were founded. The Christian school, from the moment it first appears, claims to be able to give the child everything which it needs to know for its particular age. It takes over the child.[75]

Thus, one trait of Christian education that Durkheim finds to be praise-worthy and desirable of replication in his day is its concern with the fundamental unity of the personality: "For us, too, the principal aim is not to give the child a more or less large number of pieces of knowledge, but to imbue in him some deep and internal state of mind, a kind of orientation of the social which points it in a definite direction."[76] The teacher, then, is ascribed the religious function of the formation of character and social being.

Another trait Durkheim proposes for the teacher is an emphasis on understanding, explication, and clarity of analysis. (Once again, we see Durkheim continuing his dialectic commitment to education as socialization and as scientific reflection on socialization.) Durkheim begins his course on the history of secondary education in France by asserting that the crisis of education in his time is related to the need for a faith.[77] However, he immediately adds that such a faith cannot be based on decrees and regulations. Rather, it must be "proposed, planned, published, and in some way pleaded for by informed opinion";[78] it cannot be created and controlled through the medium of officialdom:

> Ideals cannot be legislated into existence; they must be understood, loved, and striven for by those whose duty is to realize them. Thus, there is no task more urgent than that of helping future secondary school teachers to reach a consensus as to what is to become of the education for which they will be responsible. . . . Now there is no way of achieving this other than by confronting future teachers with the questions which arise and with the reasons why they arise, by equipping them with all the pieces of factual knowledge which might help them in reaching solutions to the problems, and by guiding their reflections with liberal teaching methods. . . . It is not a question of simply instructing our future teachers in how to apply a number of sound recipes. They must be confronted with the problems of secondary school culture in its entirety. This is precisely what the course of study we are going to begin this year seeks to achieve.[79]

Indeed, Durkheim's course on the history of secondary education may be seen as an exemplar of the notion of teaching that he espouses.[80] It combined moments of passion, poetry, faith, and religious language, with a patient, detailed analysis of educational institutions in terms of their broad social contexts. Durkheim's lectures on the topic were, on one hand, clearly aimed at people going into the practical world of the classroom, and as such they had to be alive, "practical," and inspiring (the teacher as a priest and bearer of the "gospel of society"). At the same time, they were to be concerned with clarity, reasons, and proofs and to prepare themselves to be on "guard against transmitting the moral gospels of our elders as a sort of closed book."[81]

These qualities combine to delineate a complicated model of the moral teacher as encompassing authority, a quasi-religious faith and passion, and reflection. The Durkheimian model of the teacher assumes the feasibility of the combined existence of these factors; post-Durkheimian conceptions of the role of the teacher in moral education have usually opted for *one* of those three elements as the essential trait, and rarely have they conceived of them as a composite entity.

PEDAGOGY

The nature of Durkheim's academic position also leads him to confront issues directly related to the world of pedagogy. In this context, Durkheim devotes time to the meta-issue of the nature of pedagogy. He talks about three distinct categories:[82]

1. Education — "the influence exerted on children by parents and teachers"
2. The science of education — the description and explanation of "the influence exercised by one generation on the following generation"
3. Pedagogy — "theories about ways of conceiving of education, especially ways of reflecting on the phenomena of education."

'Education' is the actual practice of exerting influence on children; 'science' explains and measures what has been or is in the world of education; 'pedagogy' comes to reflect on practice and suggest what should be done. Pedagogy is, then, neither art nor science, but rather a unique intermediate stage that is characterized by "reflection on the processes of ideas."[83] While not purely scientific nor deducible from science, pedagogy is rooted in the constant intelligent and reflective reexamination and adjustment of education.

In his own work with teachers on the subject of moral education, Durkheim was interested mainly in this sphere of intelligent and reflective reexamination, rather than in specific didactic recipes or prescriptions. Indeed, he warns against the conversion of educational practice into mechanical habits: "Now the only way to prevent education from falling under the yoke of habit and from degenerating into mechanical and immutable automatism is to keep it constantly adaptable by reflection."[84] Indeed, his main concern seems to be with engaging the teacher in the process of reflection on educational practice.

There are, however, some very practical comments on procedure and methodology of moral education in Durkheim, especially in Part II of the course on Moral Education ("How to Develop the Elements of Morality in the Child"). This section is a potpourri of theoretical and practical comments on moral education.

One of the first practical comments in this context is Durkheim's strong affirmation of the centrality of state, public education for moral education. His position is a response to the critics of his day (and ours) who doubt the viability or legitimacy of the role of the public school in the domain of moral education. Durkheim argues that both structurally and ideologically, state schools are equipped to do moral education.

Durkheim posits three central elements to a pedagogy of moral education: the teacher, the social context, and the subject matter of the curriculum. As we have already noted, in this scheme the teacher's authority is a key means of developing the sense of duty so crucial to the moral life. The authority of the teacher is both a way of transmitting the value of order and keeping order in the classroom. At the same time, such authority must be used benevolently:

> The teacher's authority should then be tempered with benevolence so that firmness never degenerates into boorishness or harshness.[85]

> The teacher must be sensitive to the fragility of the organism — the child — placed in his hands.[86]

The best pedagogic device for developing the social element of moral education, according to Durkheim, is through the utilization of the class as a social group.[87] Thus, he encourages the emphasis of the development of class spirit, loyalty to the class, the class as a home. The most desirable means for developing autonomy, the third component of morality, is through the formal teaching of specific subjects. The formal curriculum is, in fact, an important aspect of the Durkheimian approach to moral education and is aimed at "actually giving the child a sense of the real complexity of things."[88] Such formal teaching should focus on the analysis and explication of process and events of history and life via the subjects of science, history, and sociology.

CONCLUSION

This discussion of Emile Durkheim's system of moral education is an appropriate first stop on our journey. His work is the outcome of three unique inputs: (1) the long tradition of moral philosophy in which he was steeped and to which he reacted, (2) his pioneering effort to create a new approach to the study of man and society, and (3) his lifelong involvement with the world of education. The theory of moral education that emerges becomes a touchstone to which, knowingly or not, most contemporary approaches to moral education respond and react. Durkheim's theory of moral education raises the questions that have become the preoccupation and agenda of the most contemporary theories and practices of moral education.

Chapter 3

JOHN WILSON: MORAL EDUCATION AS RATIONAL UTILITARIANISM

ONE OF THE UNIQUE CONTRIBUTIONS to the discussion of moral education in the past two decades has been made by the British philosopher of education, John Wilson. Wilson developed a theory of moral education that is rooted in philosophy and aimed at educational practice. Whereas Durkheim begins with sociology, values clarification with educational practice, and Kohlberg with empirical research on children's development, Wilson's conception of moral education is rooted in a careful and comprehensive philosophic infrastructure. In this chapter we shall examine the contents of his theory as well as his meta-assumption concerning philosophy as the keystone for the determination of a theory of moral education.[1]

THE SOCIAL AND THE INDIVIDUAL

In the opening section of *Introduction to Moral Education*, Wilson makes the following distinction between uses of the term 'moral':

> A. 'Moral' (as contrasted with 'immoral'), is often used as a term of approval.
> B. 'Moral' is used as a descriptive term, to classify a particular kind of action or belief. Its opposite here is simply 'not moral' or 'non-moral' (as when we say, "It's not a moral issue, it's simply a matter of taste").[2]

The 'B' sense of 'moral' (i.e., its descriptive or classificatory sense) can be further subdivided:

> (i) It can be used in a 'sociological' sense. Sociologists and historians commonly talk about 'the morality' of a particular society or social group, about what counted as 'moral' or 'immoral' behavior in ancient Sparta or during the Victorian age in England. Here we refer to a particular code or set of *mores*. When we use these words with reference to our own society we often bring in a sense 'A' above, with its overtones of praise or blame: we say "that's a

29

most immoral thing to do," meaning that it is against the current moral code, and probably also implying our condemnation of the action.

(ii) It can be used to mark out a particular kind of human thought and action, not on the basis of what the *mores* of a particular society are, but on some other basis. Thus when we say "The ancient Hebrews thought that whether or not you ate certain kinds of food was a moral issue, but I don't think it is" or "What sort of clothes you wear isn't really a moral issue, it's a matter of taste," we are obviously not thinking just of what the *mores* of a particular society are. We seem rather to be making some kind of logical or conceptual classification of the area of morality, quite apart from what anyone *regards* (rightly or wrongly) as that area.[3]

One of the main concerns of John Wilson is to present a notion of morality and moral education that falls into category B (ii) rather than B(i). Wilson is concerned with the presentation of a notion of morality as a *procedure* for confronting moral issues, rather than as a set of mores of a particular society to be inculcated in the young. Indeed, Wilson is a prominent figure in a movement in contemporary moral education that is concerned about shifting the emphasis from the transmission of specific values and mores to the development of individual inquiry and moral deliberation. His concern is to develop a series of abilities in individuals ("the moral components") that will enable them to personally confront and resolve moral dilemmas without the dictate of some outside force.

This approach constitutes a renewed commitment to the role of the individual and increased doubt and hesitance vis à vis social dominance in morality. Wilson proposes to penetrate the social and institutional dimensions of morality (and religion) so as to isolate its generic individual basis. Wilson's approach is neither asocial nor antisocial; that is, it does not deny the social context nor the responsibility that characterize morality. However, his theory is a strong argument for the centrality of the autonomous individual in the moral drama.

There are those who argue that Wilson's notion of morality is inherently more social—and perhaps even conventional—than it would seem.[4] First, Wilson posits the existence of a "fraternal instinct" and "need for communication in people," and he suggests that lack of fulfillment of this instinct, in fact, leads to impaired mental health.[5] Thus, the social concern would seem to be a basic instinctual force for him. Second, the concern for others and for treating them as equals (PHIL) is one of the basic moral components or constituents of the moral process according to Wilson. (See the next section for a further description of PHIL.) The very process of moral thinking is defined by and oriented to the concern for others. Third, Wilson's practical discussions of how we actually carry out moral education present a surprisingly detailed description of and commitment to social contexts as the means for moral education.[6] Thus, the apparently individual-centered Wilsonian model is complicated by both a theoretical and a practical emphasis on social dimensions of morality and moral education. This feature has led some commentators to argue that Wilson actually postulates two moralities: (1) a rationalistic-utilitarian one of universal values whose acceptance is a necessary condition of civilized social life and complementary to rationality, and (2) a morality of personal ideals which is essentially a matter of choice and not entirely susceptible of rational discussion.[7] However, the answer does not seem to be in the notion of two moralities for Wilson; rather, what we in fact find in this theory is a radically different conception of the relationship of the individual to society than we found in Durkheim. Durkheim begins with the assumption of society as the starting point and as the creator of individuals; for him 'society' is an ontological category. For Wilson, the individual is the starting point and he enters into 'social contracts' for both instinctual and pragmatic reasons. Individuals create societies to fulfill certain needs or demands. Thus, societies are part of morality as preconditions and contexts, but they in themselves are not moral phenomena; instead, the heart of the moral process is related to autonomous moral deliberation.

Therefore, morality is not inherently social, even though it takes place in and is arrived at in social contexts. The true morality is linked to the domain of the individual and his/her confrontation with universalizable moral principles.

MORAL PRINCIPLES

The second major theme of John Wilson is his emphasis on morality as a principled act. Wilson's work is a response to and reaction against a conception of moral education that deemphasizes principles and principled action in the moral sphere.[8] Wilson is concerned with the development of agents who choose moral behavior on the basis of the reflective confrontation with a body of overriding and universalizable moral principles. Moral principles are emphasized in two parts of Wilson's taxonomy of moral components. First, principles are a key dimension of PHIL ('the concern for others', 'sympathy', 'a sense of fair play', 'respect for other people'); PHIL has three dimensions:

PHIL (HC) — Having the concept of a 'person'.
PHIL (CC) — Claiming to use this concept in an overriding, prescriptive, and universalized (O, P, and U) principle.
PHIL (RSF) (DO and PO) — Having feelings that support this prin-

ciple, either of a 'duty-oriented' (DO) or a 'person-oriented' (PO) kind.

PHIL (CC) means to claim concern for others as a "moral principle", that is, as "an overriding, prescriptive and universalized principle".[9] Thus, one crucial sense in which someone is 'moral', according to Wilson, is if he has PHIL, and regards it or accepts it as a moral principle.

Second, the concept KRAT refers to the general process of thinking about and deciding on moral issues on the basis of the concern for others (PHIL), a sense of feeling for others or one's own interests (EMP), certain basic knowledge and skill related to the issue (GIG). Specifically, in KRAT (1) OPU the individual thinks about a situation and makes a decision that is *overriding, prescriptive*, and *universalizable* — a principled decision: "KRAT (1) (OPU) — as a result of the foregoing making an overriding, prescriptive, and universalized decision to act in others' interests."[10]

Indeed, it can be argued that Wilson's entire system of moral education is on the level of principles. He is concerned with a person's ability to 'do morality'; that is, to employ the components and tools necessary for the person to operate in the field of morality. These various components and tools are, in effect, generalizable, nonspecific categories, which, if utilized, mean that the individual has set into motion the principles of operating as a moral being.

Wilson argues that he is not prescribing a specific set of moral principles, but rather, that he is engaged in the second-order activity of describing the logic of morality.[11] His contention is that his moral components are logical constructs, rather than a particular 'moral' theory of 'good' or 'right'.[12] Wilson's contention that he presents a morally neutral notion of moral principles has been the subject of much discussion and criticism in the literature:[13] Despite his disclaimers, it is obvious that such principled rationalism is, in fact, a particular theory of morality, and it represents one powerful school of moral philosophy:[14]

> Despite his protestations, they are strongly partisan and pervaded by a zealous proselytizing spirit which seems to bring his readers to espouse his own starry-eyed (his words not mine) way of looking at the world. He seems to cultivate by what he calls 'moral education' a commitment to other people's interests and to induce people to regard others as equals.[15]

> Some of what he calls second-order norms or procedural principles (e.g., treating people as equals and considering their interests) are, in fact, first-order norms formulated in a very general way.[16]

The heart of the problem relates to PHIL, which Wilson claims is a

logical, formal concept and which his critics claim is substantive and normative. Wilson presents several formulations of PHIL in his works:

> *Introduction to Moral Education*: The degree to which one can identify with
> the people in the sense of being such that other people's feelings and interests
> actually count or weigh with one.[17]
>
> *Education in Religion and the Emotions*: An *attitude*, respect/concern for
> others.[18]
>
> *Moral Thinking*: Regarding other people as equals, thinking that other peo-
> ple's interests count.[19]
>
> *The Assessment of Morality*: Under the heading PHIL we have to make sense
> of the area often described in such terms as 'concern for others', 'sympathy',
> 'sense of fair play', 'respect for other people' . . . we have distinguished three
> subcomponents of PHIL:
>
>   (1) having the concept of a 'person'. I shall call this PHIL (HC).
>   (2) claiming the concept as a moral principle: PHIL (CC).
>   (3) having rule-supported feelings, 'duty-oriented' or 'person-oriented': PHIL
>   (RSF-DO).[20]

In all these formulations, the interests of others are central, and constitute
the decisive criterion of morality for Wilson. In that sense, it is claimed
that Wilson, in fact, espouses a specific normative ethic of the rational-
utilitarian model. The argument is that PHIL reflects a particular notion
of human nature, which, among other things, assumes that man "has certain basic desires which are the desire for relationship based on fraternal
communication" and the desire and ability to be concerned for others.

Thus, the critics claim that under the guise of logical analysis, Wilson
has actually interjected a particular (admittedly powerful) theory of human
nature and morality. Indeed, they argue, Wilson is guilty of one of the very
evils that he as an analytic philosopher of education so often attacks, namely the use of philosophy to promulgate certain normative stances: "Wilson
has taken the political statement 'the rationality of treating others' and then
tried to turn it into an analytic philosophic statement."[21]

Wilson has frequently responded to his critics, repeating the claim that
his ethic is formal rather than normative.[22] However, a careful look at the
three dimensions of PHIL seems to lend credence to the critics' position.
The first dimension of PHIL (HC) is, as Wilson claims, nonnormative:
"It is important that we should remember what is meant by 'having a conception of'. As I use the phrase, it will refer solely to S's ability to conceive of all 'people' as forming one class, and (given the facts) to identify
any 'person' as a member of that class."[23]

Assuming for the moment that people do form one class and have qualities that so identify them as members of one class, this subcomponent may indeed be formal. The other two subcomponents of PHIL are not, however, of the same order. PHIL (CC) refers to turning the principle of the worth of others into an overriding, prescriptive, and universalizable principle, and PHIL (RSF-DO) refers to the holding of feelings that support the principle of a duty as a 'person' orientation. PHIL (CC) and PHIL (RSF-DO + PO) encompass having a positive feeling toward the principle of concern for others and having a disposition to act in accordance with this principle. PHIL in toto clearly involves the sense that concern for others is right and should be acted upon. Indeed, PHIL is the most normative of components; it reflects a certain view of man and of the good. It enunciates a clear, substantive, moral position. It regards such a (substantive) moral position as indispensable to the (logical) methodology of carrying out morality.

Thus, Wilson's approach argues for the importance of the principled person in the moral sphere, but it also prescribes a specific content or substance for such a principled life, that is, the consideration of other people's interests. At this point, the discussion reverts to the long-standing philosophic discussion vis à vis the desirable contents or principles of morality.[24] Thus, some philosophic positions certainly would agree with 'others' interests' as the best criterion for moral principles. However, as Mary Warnock reminds us, there are other virtues that have also been considered as legitimate and/or overriding, for example, truthfulness, generosity, and honesty. Thus, once the cover of neutrality has been removed from Wilson's analysis of moral principles, the discussion then becomes not about a logic of morality, but rather about utilitarianism as a moral theory.[25]

Wilson's discussion of the moral person as principled is an important contribution to the contemporary literature on moral education, and an important counterbalance to prevailing theory and practice. His system clearly details the place of principles in the process of 'doing morality'. Its deficiencies also inform us, and they ironically seem to suggest the pedagogic conclusion that we ultimately teach *how* to be a principled person in the moral sphere by actually presenting specific moral principles and their use (e.g., as Wilson does with PHIL). The goal or outcome need not be that the child necessarily accepts the specific principle; however, the procedure of doing morality probably cannot be taught without the input of specific principles. When seen in this light, we can argue that *it is* accurate to speak of the second-order nature of Wilson's system, and that in that sense it certainly focuses on the teaching of methodology. Wilson's fallacy is the assumption that methodology and content are distinguishable and that we can educate for the former without the latter.

REASON IN ETHICS

A third philosophic task of Wilson is to argue against the notion of morality as an expression of taste or a question of feeling and to defend the conception of morality as part of the sphere of rational discourse. Wilson aligns himself from the outset with the neocognitivist position of R. M. Hare, which characterizes morality as universalizable, prescriptive, and principled thought and action. 'Being rational' in the moral sphere for Wilson means:[26]

1. Acting for a reason.
2. Acting for a reason related to other people's interests.
3. Being logically consistent.
4. Knowing the facts and facing them.
5. Applying all these skills and translating them into action.

Wilson's notion of moral reasoning first implies being consistent in the use of language and agreed-upon procedures of connecting words and concepts. Second, it involves the reference to principles — as generalizable prescriptive statements — in the process of making a decision. Third, it includes reference to empirically verifiable 'facts'; to reason morally includes utilization of the best conclusions of the sciences — social and natural. Fourth, moral reasoning is rooted in the individual's own freely chosen reflection and deliberation; it must be autonomous and intentional. Finally, moral reasoning includes the consideration of options and choices in terms of their implications for the interests of others; that is, the principle of others' interests is one of the defining characteristics of Wilson's process of moral reasoning.

Wilson proposes to clarify his conception of moral thinking by juxtaposing it with some unsatisfactory approaches to solving moral problems:[27]

1. Acceptance of an outside authority that tells us what to do.
2. Reference to certain ideal people (Martin Luther King, Socrates, Jesus) who serve as exemplars of how we should behave.
3. Faith — acceptance of a set of Beliefs or Truths that determine how we should act.
4. Regarding moral decisions simply as a matter of personal preference.
5. Deciding and acting in terms of the way we were brought up.
6. Being influenced by certain special events or experiences that have had a charismatic effect on our lives.
7. Our morality being determined by what other people say or do.

Wilson's position, then, implies the existence of an objective, nonnormative procedure of reasoning that can be applied in ethics, much as such procedures are applied in mathematics or the sciences.

Wilson's theory of moral reasoning raises several questions. Some critics have doubted Wilson's claim as to the second-order, procedural nature of his conception of reason in ethics:

> Some of what Wilson calls second-order norms or procedural principles in morality (e.g., the procedure of treating people as equals and considering their interests) are *in fact* first-order *norms* formulated in a very general way.[28]

> Despite Wilson's disclaimers, it is obvious that such rationalism is in fact a particular theory of morality. It represents one powerful school of moral philosophy.[29]

Wilson's critics have argued with the claim that his notion of moral thinking is a nonnormative, neutral phenomenon such that "any sane and sensible person" would accept it;[30] rather, they contend, this notion of moral reasoning implies an *a priori* acceptance of some first-order principles. Thus, as we have seen, Wilson's PHIL is categorically a form of 'faith statement' that implies some belief in man's benevolent nature, rather than a logically characteristic quality. His notion of a procedure of morality actually reflects prior assumptions which do *not* evoke the agreement that Wilson posits and which have elicited much argument in the history of moral philosophy; indeed, many "sane and sensible people" have vehemently disagreed about the nature of moral reasoning, and it is not a topic about which there is unanimity or consensus in philosophy.

Thus, this critique shifts the focus of discussion from Wilson's claims of a metatheory of morality to the prior question of the validity of the substantive theory of moral reasoning that he presents. Even if we grant that Wilson's notion of moral reasoning may be less procedural and neutral than he claims, the larger question is whether it is a sound or defensible conception of moral reasoning.

Wilson's critics take issue with him on this point also. Warnock argues that Wilson's theory is inadequate because it is reductionist, since morality encompasses virtue as well as the consideration of others' interests.[31] Wilson, she suggests, underestimates and simplifies the nature of morality. Stafford suggests that it is not clear that autonomous, rational deliberation is necessarily better than conventional-but-decent human behaviors. That is, the ability to freely enunciate moral justifications is not necessarily better than being acted upon by efficient causes. Indeed, a person who is brought up to consider other people's interests and who acts upon that principle as an adult might be as 'moral' as one who operationalized autonomous moral thinking. The critics, then, suggest that the prior assumptions of Wilson's theory are less definitive or agreed upon than Wilson would have us believe.

Wilson's theory of moral education, as concerned with rational and autonomous man is, of course, a reaction against certain philosophical and educational schools which have abrogated the role of self and mind in the moral sphere. His notion of the centrality of reason to moral education constitutes rejection of this theory and a defense of an alternative theory. Wilson's critics remind us that while his theory is to be taken seriously, it is not as apparent as we might think. Indeed, if Wilson is correct that we have the ability to reflect on moral matters, then surely there is room to ponder the reasonableness of the theory which he himself proposes.

FORM-CONTENT

We have seen that Wilson's approach to moral education purports to be about the teaching of a procedure or a methodology, and not about the teaching of specific moral values or contents. As noted, Wilson's emphasis reflects a prominent thrust of much of contemporary theory of moral education; namely, the movement away from a notion of moral education as the teaching of specific moral values or behaviors, and towards an emphasis on the general ability to confront problems in the moral sphere. Thus, it would seem that Wilson takes a clear stance on morality as essentially a formal phenomenon. Our previous discussion of Wilson has clearly suggested some problems with the notion of morality as process and indeed with the process-content bifurcation. Wilson's process proves to be significantly determined by a specific moral content — that is, concern for other's interests. Hence, in his case at least, the discussion of morality as a process similar to swimming or driving or weaving is not appropriate. Learning to drive does involve the internalization of a series of skills and reflexes which a person can utilize subsequently to apply to the act of driving a car (or different cars) to various places or objectives. The skill of driving a car does not necessarily determine the routes to be taken or the places to be visited in the car. However, Wilson's notion of the moral process does seem to predetermine a route and to imply a certain substantive moral point of view. Thus, this process is less procedural than Wilson would have us believe.

There is another aspect to Wilson's process emphasis that seems to be more convincing. Morality, says Wilson, is not a series of specific responses or reactions, but rather a generalized approach to confronting problems. He argues against the reduction of morality to specific answers and actions; instead, it encompasses a general point of view. The emphasis in this instance is on the *general* rather than the *nonnormative* nature of the process of morality. Wilson emphasizes morality as a procedure that we learn and then apply to a broad range of moral situations. Thus, it is the trait of broad applicability rather than objectivity that, in fact, may be Wilson's contribution to the discussion of morality as process.

ACTION

Wilson's theory of moral education shares the concern with moral action that characterizes several classical and contemporary schools of moral philosophy. However, Wilson's approach does not reflect the polarization of some approaches of morality into either thought or action; rather, Wilson's approach is committed to the unity of knowing and doing in the moral sphere. Wilson's moral components are intimately interrelated with each other, and they are synthesized via the component of KRAT to lead to moral action. Wilson's model is an affirmation of the multidimensional nature of morality, and of its indivisibility and irreducibility. Wilson's system is ultimately concerned with the way in which "knowing," "feeling," and "doing" form one whole in the moral sphere. (Wilson once used the terms 'attitudes', 'knowledge', and 'behaviors' to talk about the components; however, he later rejected the description of his components via these terms.) Thus, the classical and modern question as to whether *knowing* leads to *doing* is not an issue for Wilson, since his system is about education in *all* of those elements crucial to being moral.[32]

Indeed, the various elements of Wilson's system fit together into one of the more rigorous and internally logical contemporary systems of moral education. Wilson uses assumptions, terms, and linguistic procedures in a consistent fashion within specific analyses and *across* different analyses. (Consequently, our treatments in these sections flow into and from each other and, indeed, at certain points even repeat themselves.) Moreover, this same consistency exists throughout Wilson's other writings on education, even when they do not specifically or solely relate to the moral domain.[33] Thus, while Wilson is very much in the modern tradition in philosophy that has attempted to shed the mantle of system building, his work is a rather striking example of integration and synthesis of ideas into a unified whole.

THE CONCEPTION OF THE MORALLY EDUCATED PERSON

Wilson presents a detailed picture of the components of the morally educated person, which fall into four general categories (PHIL, EMP, GIG, and KRAT) and sixteen subcategories:

[a]	PHIL (HC)	Having the concept of a 'person'.
[b]	PHIL (CC)	Claiming to use this concept in an overriding, prescriptive, and universalized (O, P, and U) principle.
[c]	PHIL (RSF) (DO & PO)	Having feelings that support this principle, either of a 'duty-oriented' (DO) or a 'person-oriented' (PO) kind.
[d(i)]	EMP (HC)	Having the concepts of various emotions (moods, etc.).
[d(i)]	EMP (1) (Cs)	Being able, in practice, to identify emotions, etc. in oneself, when these are at a conscious level.
[d(i)]	EMP (1) (Ucs)	Ditto, when the emotions are at an unconscious level.
[d(i)]	EMP (2) (Cs)	Ditto, in other people, when at a conscious level.
[d(i)]	EMP (2) (Ucs)	Ditto, when at an unconscious level.
[d(ii)]	GIG (1) (KF)	Knowing other ('hard') facts relevant to moral decisions.
[d(ii)]	GIG (1) (KS)	Knowing sources of facts (where to find out) as above.
[e]	GIG (2) (VC)	'Knowing how' — a 'skill' element in dealing with moral situations, as evinced in verbal communications with others.
[e]	GIG (2) (NVC)	Ditto, in nonverbal communication.
[f(i)]	KRAT (1) (RA)	Being, in practice, 'relevantly alert' to (noticing) moral situations, and seeing them as such (describing them in terms of PHIL, etc.).
[f(ii)]	KRAT (1) (TT)	Thinking thoroughly about such situations, and bringing to bear what PHIL, EMP, and GIG we have.
[f(iii)]	KRAT (1) (OPU)	As a result of the foregoing, making an overriding, prescriptive, and universalized decision to act in others' interests.
[g]	KRAT (2)	Being sufficiently wholehearted, free from unconscious countermotivation, etc. to carry out (when able) the decision arrived at in practice.[34]

In early writings, Wilson calls these components 'abilities' or 'mechanisms', but in later versions, he has difficulties in finding the right noun to describe them, and he rejects a long list of terms, for example, 'psychological entities', 'factors', 'forces', 'mechanisms', 'innate abilities', 'capacities', 'competencies', 'motivations', 'attainments'.[35] He suggests that we can best understand the status of these components if they are seen in the context of the following question: "Is it true of S that . . . ?" That is, the components are phenomena, and with them we are able to do, feel, identify, know, and perform certain types of things. What is valuable in Wilson's admittedly complicated and frustrating reservations about the status of the components is its emphasis on the multifaceted, nonreducible nature of being moral. The educational implication is, of course, that to educate for the moral person is a multidimensional, multiprocedural, and probably very long process.

Wilson's notion of the components of the morally educated person is obviously different from the traits of the morally socialized or well-behaved child. His model, as that of Kohlberg or values clarification, presents a whole new bag of educational problems related to pedagogy and evaluation. Wilson's notion of the moral person implies techniques and tests that have to measure behaviors, feelings, reasoning processes, value stances, and factual and conceptual knowledge. Thus, on one hand, as a new model it does not yet offer a rich bank of educational techniques to exemplify it. On the other hand, it is a system that seems to suggest a plethora of educational practices derived from a theoretical superstructure.[36]

INDOCTRINATION

Wilson has dealt with the concept of 'indoctrination' in two contexts: a paper on "Education and Indoctrination" and a section of *Introduction to Moral Education*.[37] In the former, Wilson aligns himself with an approach to 'indoctrination' that defines it in terms of its contents, specifically, in terms of the presentation of certain kinds of subjects or materials that are less than rational in the following sense: "It is not true that any sane and sensible person, when presented with the relevant facts and arguments would necessarily hold the belief"; therefore, indoctrination refers to the teaching of beliefs for which "there is no publicly accepted evidence . . . evidence which any rational person would regard as sufficient."[38]

R. M. Hare has responded to Wilson's position by casting doubt on the phrases "a sane and sensible person" and "rational beliefs".[39] Hare asks who is to be counted as a sane and sensible person, and what makes some beliefs 'rational' and others not? Hare's point is that Wilson presupposes the notion of a fixed, agreed-upon set of criteria that make some subjects 'rational' (e.g., mathematics or grammar). Indeed, Wilson may well have misrepresented himself in the Hollins volume, and aligned himself in a somewhat inaccurate fashion with the content approach to defining moral education — when, in fact, he is actually closer to the 'aims' school. In the earlier article, Wilson claims that the criteria of indoctrination depend upon the rationality of the *content* of what is taught, but at the same time he emphasizes the importance of evidence, giving reasons, and rational procedures in education. That is, he really seems to be concerned with what is done with certain contents, in what ways they are being taught, and for what purposes.

This thrust becomes more evident in his discussion of 'indoctrination' in *Introduction to Moral Education*, where the focus shifts from the nature of the beliefs held to the purposes that underlie the teaching of such beliefs. Thus, he now describes 'indoctrination' as illegitimately implanting a belief in children, or as the unfair presentation of reasons for a belief (e.g., "stacking the deck").[40] Wilson distinguishes between 'indoctrination', 'conditioning', and 'force', indicating that indoctrination is not a totally compulsory or will-less activity, and that reasons are present in it. The indoctrinated person has beliefs for which reasons can be given; the problem is that such reasons have been acquired in an inferior manner. Indeed, one of the keystones of Wilson's approach to moral education is that people should be free to reflect on and choose their own moral commitments. In later writings, morality and religion are no longer treated by Wilson as "irrational" subjects; indeed, he now goes to great pains to argue that morality is a "subject with a logic of its own and it is even of such a level that it should be taught directly as a regular topic in schools."[41] Thus, Wilson moves from defining 'indoctrination' as the teaching of morality or religion *per se* to a notion of 'indoctrination' as the teaching of such (and other subjects) in a way that prevents the child from being an independent, reflective, and decision-making moral agent (i.e., a person with PHIL, EMP, GIG, and KRAT). Needless to say, Wilson has remained throughout an avid foe of 'indoctrination', and has continually assumed the affective distinction between 'education' as implying favorable activities and 'indoctrination' as implying unfavorable activities. He now views 'indoctrination' as unfavorable not because of what it teaches, but rather because of what it tries to do to children.

THE TEACHER

The teacher is a central figure in Wilson's approach to moral education, and the essence of his/her role is to aid in the development of the moral components in the learner. In order to engage in this task, the teacher must develop (1) the philosophic understanding of the theoretical underpinnings of the components and (2) the practical ability to develop and teach instructional units that convey the components. Thus, Wilson asks his teacher to be philosophically thoughtful and pedagogically proficient; in that sense, morality implies for Wilson a precisely defined subject area that requires appropriate substantive and pedagogic expertise. Wilson does not regard the teacher's primary role as the exemplar of socially desirable behaviors, advocate of some specific bag of moral values, facilitator of group process, or catalyst for moral introspection. The philosophic rigor of Wilson's system and the pedagogic role he assigns to the teacher do not imply that morality is to be regarded as a mystical, inaccessible legacy of the few or that morality is reserved for an intellectual elite. Wilson believes that the philosophic reflection on and understanding of morality is accessible to the normal teacher; indeed, one of his major pedagogic thrusts is to help teachers engage in and master such philosophic deliberation.

At the same time, Wilson joins Mary Warnock in doubting the legitimacy of the neutral teacher in the sphere of moral education.[42] They both contend that one of the (formal) characteristics of making a moral decision is "taking a stand," and being neutral means to deny students the opportunity of observing the complete process of moral deliberation. Thus, it is not enough for teachers to present evidence; they must help children distinguish between "good" and "bad" evidence and show them how to draw conclusions from evidence to general theses. Hence, in order to teach the process of value deliberation and resolution, a teacher *must* reveal a viewpoint. To be neutral or passive in this context is to miseducate and to prevent the child from seeing the entire process of value deliberation and decision making. Since morality (and religion) involves reasoning that leads to decisions, then "students should not be deprived of the spectacle of a teacher who holds or clearly expresses moral views".[43] Thus, the teacher demonstrates a process and in so doing expresses a moral stance at the same time.

PEDAGOGY

Wilson's approach to moral education has not resulted in the development of an extensive body of classroom materials, games, filmstrips, teaching units, and textbooks. This fact partially accounts for Wilson's lack of impact on educational practice as compared with that of values clarification or Kohlberg. Moreover, it is unlikely that an extensive collection of practical materials would ever be produced by Wilson, since he is ultimately suggesting an alternative notion for the pedagogy of moral education that assumes that the subject matter of moral education is morality and that the key pedagogic task is to teach teachers to understand morality so that they themselves can create appropriate materials.

At the same time, Wilson's writings do refer to the types of educational procedures that he regards as consistent with his approach. Wilson urges a systematic teaching about the moral sphere or about moral thinking as part of any school curriculum.[44] Such teaching may be effected via regular courses in 'morality', which would concentrate on the analysis and explication of the moral components; such courses would be exercises in 'moral philosophy' rather than 'moralizing'. They could be separate subjects in the school curriculum, or they could be integrated into other subject areas in a way that would focus on moral components. History and literature could be used to increase awareness of other people in society; mime and drama could be used to objectify moral problems; and music and art are relevant for showing the ways in which emotions are expressed.[45]

Wilson emphasizes the importance of the dialectic method in the various contexts of moral education in schools. Dialectic is important for the involvement and the tension that it generates; it causes the student to become personally involved with moral issues and to deal with them in a passionate and nonpassive manner.

There is a surprisingly un-Wilsonian minor leitmotif that surfaces in some of his more practical works on moral education in which he advocates a moral education for norms transmission, for the development of specific behavioral traits, and for preserving the social order.[46] How are we to explain this apparently Durkheimian melody in an otherwise normal Wilsonian symphony? Wilson himself clarifies the paradox by distinguishing between two types of school-based activities: 'moral education' and 'preconditions for moral education'.

'Moral education' refers to the development of the rational, autonomous, moral person who is the subject of the bulk of his writings. The development of such a person should be the goal of schools. 'Preconditions for moral education' refer to activities that are necessary before the individual can become the rational moral person; the preconditions include such qualities as the ability to have a sense of self-esteem, the experiencing of meaningful personal relationships, and the skill of confronting others' feelings. Preconditions are not themselves moral components, but they are necessary prior factors in the process of rational development. Thus, Wilson's rational moral education often includes traditional moral socialization.

Wilson's pedagogy, in fact, proves to be quite structured, curricularized, and often surprisingly convention oriented. Indeed, as Wilson comes closer to the classroom, he sometimes begins to look like his French colleague of several decades ago.

SUMMARY

John Wilson differs from some of the others in this discussion by virtue of his roots in a prominent classical and contemporary philosophic tradition. His model of moral education is a prominent example of a deductive educational theory in which educational practice is preceded by and derived from a carefully developed, holistic, philosophic conception. His work reveals both the promise and the limitations of philosophy for educational practice.

Chapter 4

MORAL EDUCATION AS VALUES CLARIFICATION

VALUES CLARIFICATION (often denoted by its initials, VC) is among the most popular of the "new" approaches to moral education. It is easily understandable; it presents some clear and convincing arguments for its validity; teachers can quickly learn how to do it; it usually is enjoyable and interesting for students; and there are scores of VC books, filmstrips, exercises, and workshops, which make it easily accessible.[1]

The elucidation of VC's underlying philosophic and educational theory is a more complicated exercise than the analysis of Durkheim or Wilson. First, despite periodic references to theoretical forefathers, VC, in fact, developed in a much more inductive, pragmatic, and experimental fashion than Wilson or Durkheim. It is an approach that did not begin with a fully developed, comprehensive, philosophic theory that was then translated into practical terms; rather, it is an evolving compendium of assumptions about educational values that may or may not actually constitute an organic theory. Second, VC has not had one exclusive spokesman or theoretician. Louis Raths is credited as being the senior author and central figure in the original statement of VC.[2] Subsequently, Sidney Simon, Merrill Harmin, Howard Kirschenbaum, and others have together and separately published collections of VC exercises and theoretical statements.

The various versions of VC have not always been the same. Indeed, I shall argue in this chapter that there are actually *two* versions of VC: the first version (which I shall call VC₁) is best represented by the early statement of Raths, Harmin, and Simon in *Values and Teaching*, and the second version (to be denoted as VC₂) is best represented by Kirschenbaum's work, particularly his two essays "Beyond Values Clarification" (1973), and "Clarifying Values Clarification: Some Theoretical Issues" (1976).[3]

Thus, in order to explicate VC, we shall have to employ an analytic technique somewhat different from that used vis à vis Durkheim and Wilson. In this instance, we shall have to relate to a much more disparate and heterogeneous body of articles and literature, including both theoretical statements and practical exercises. Moreover, we shall have to infer much more than in previous cases; both Wilson and Durkheim present detailed statements and explications of their theoretical underpinnings, whereas VC is much more telegraphic. In addition, we shall have to distinguish between the two versions of VC that have been delineated (VC_1 = the earliest formulation of the approach; VC_2 = Kirschenbaum's formulations; VC = arguments that are common to both VC_1 and VC_2). Finally, we shall make greater use of second-order critical literature than we have in previous chapters, since we have less of a systematic primary literature to draw upon, and other attempts to delineate the implicit system of VC will be helpful for our effort.

INDIVIDUAL-SOCIAL

VC's starting point is the claim that the young person today exists in a new and complicated world of competing and confusing value perspectives, each of which comes to impose itself on the young.[4] These various perspectives are reflected in political, religious, and moral codes and ideologies that societies attempt to impose on the young. The plurality of such ideologies and the attempted imposition of them onto children by society constitute the crisis of moral education and act as the catalyst for the need for a new approach.

Proponents of VC are in this context objecting to two things: (1) the inculcation of contents about which there is no unanimous consensus and (2) the subjugation of the individual to the group in the values domain.

Indeed, one of the dominant themes throughout VC, and perhaps its most consistent message, is the personal nature of value:

> By our definition, and as we see it, by social right, values are personal things.[5]

> Values and valuing are uniquely personal dimensions of the human experience; therefore, the program itself must not suggest particular values which should be taught or acquired at specific ages, nor does it attempt to promote a curriculum for values education.[6]

Values are regarded by VC as matters of personal concern, reflection, and choice, and external forces should not be allowed to tamper with or invade this personal arena. While VC does not take the accusatory stance of Freud with respect to the inhibitory and oppressive role of society vis à vis the individual and his values, it clearly does constitute a late, twentieth-century attempt to restore the locus of influence in the value domain to what it regards as its rightful source, that is, to the individual.

VC rejects a broad range of outside forces that come to impose values: religion, social institutions, science, reason, and tradition. Its position is not that these institutions are decadent or worthless; rather, they should not be the determinants of value decisions. VC opposes any form or notion of morality as conformity to some external code or set of values or as morally conventional behavior that is exclusively determined by a social agency or institution.

There have been two characteristic critiques of values clarification on this issue. A first line of attack has focused on VC's naiveté vis à vis morality and social context. The critics argue that VC would have us assume that the seven processes that constitute valuing operate in a vacuum; whereas it would seem to be the case that valuing and morality are, in fact, intimately and inextricably linked to social contexts.[7] The contention is that VC has erred by maintaining an overly simplistic notion of the individual, as if he/she operated totally outside of social contexts. Indeed, Nevin argues that while VC claims to be in the Deweyan tradition, it is decidedly un-Deweyan on this issue, as it totally neglects Dewey's "thoroughly social notion of intelligence and valuing."[8]

A different sort of critique of VC_1 focuses on its stance against moral conventionalism. Whereas VC_1's very starting point is its attack on moral conventionalism, its critics argue that VC actually encourages and becomes an agent of such conventionalism. This paradox occurs because of VC_1's emphasis on public expression and affirmation of value preference, which, in fact, results in strong peer pressure and "coercion to the means."[9] While VC_1 posits the centrality of the individual in the valuing process, it very often provides him/her with outlandish choices and with inadequate resources for making his/her own decisions and preferences.

Kirschenbaum attempted to respond to these criticisms in his revised formulation of VC_1; specifically, he proposes to adjust the individualistic strain of VC_1 by redefining the valuing process:

> The valuing process as defined here is a process by which we increase the likelihood that our living in general or a decision in particular will first have positive value for us and second be constructive in the social context. . . . VC can be defined as an approach that utilizes questions and activities to teach the valuing process and that helps people skillfully to apply the valuing process to value-rich areas in their lives.[10]

This formulation of VC introduces the notion of the constructiveness of our value decisions for the social context. Thus, the value of decisions for the social context as well as for the individual is now emphasized. (There is a much greater use of the plural forms "we," "our," "for us," and "people" in the new formulation.)

Kirschenbaum also presents a revised formulation of the original, three-part, seven-subcategory model of VC:[11]

1966 Version (VC₁)	1975 Version (VC₂)

1966 Version (VC$_1$)

I. CHOOSING

  (1) freely
  (2) from alternatives
  (3) after thoughtful considera-
     tion of the consequences
     of each alternative

II. PRIZING

  (4) cherishing, being happy
     with the choice
  (5) enough to be willing to
     affirm the choice to others

III. ACTING

  (6) or doing something with
     the choice
  (7) repeatedly, in some pattern
     of life

1975 Version (VC$_2$)

I. THINKING

  (1) thinking on various levels
  (2) critical thinking
  (3) moral reasoning on the
     higher levels
  (4) divergent or creative
     thinking

II. FEELING

  (1) prize, cherish
  (2) feel good about oneself
  (3) aware of one's feelings

III. CHOOSING

  (1) from alternatives
  (2) considering consequences
  (3) freely
  (4) achievement planning

IV. COMMUNICATING

  (1) the ability to send clear
     messages
  (2) empathy—listening, taking
     in another's frame of
     reference
  (3) conflict resolution

V. ACTING

  (1) repeatedly
  (2) consistently
  (3) acting skillfully in the
     areas in which we act
     (competence)

Kirschenbaum introduces an entirely new category in his model, "communicating," which is about the interaction and relationship with other people. Moreover, he preferred to replace what VC$_1$ had originally called "affirming" with the word "sharing": "*Affirm* often takes on connotations of rigidity and imposition. . . . *Share* . . . suggests more of an offering — we offer our value alternative to others for their consideration."[12]

    These changes seem to imply a greater emphasis on the social context in the values domain. While the revised model certainly does not opt for a notion of society as a source of guidance or control over the values domain, it would seem to be more sensitive to the social context in which valuing takes place.

At the same time, VC_2 may also be seen as an even stronger and more radical affirmation of the centrality of the individual in valuing. Kirschenbaum is critical of VC_1's formulation of the seven components or "criteria" of the valuing process, because "the seven criteria imply an external frame of reference which seems inimical to VC. I want to use the seven valuing processes in my life because they help my inner needs find expression and fulfillment."[13] Kirschenbaum feels that VC_1 was not sensitive enough to the liberation of the individual's feelings and affect and, in fact, that it was too cognitive. VC_2 comes to expand and personalize the individual's thinking (thinking is now a separate category with four subdivisions) as well as to deepen and enrich his 'feeling' (which is the successor to VC_1's 'prizing'). What this means is that the individual is now charged with a more detailed and complex set of personal tasks and skills in the process of valuing. The "new" VC valuing person must be able to think on various levels, think critically, think divergently, set goals, collect data, consider consequences, send clear messages, empathize, and resolve conflicts. If, in fact, a person were able to operationalize all these skills, he/she would, indeed, be an individual with great mastery over his/her destiny.

What emerges in VC with respect to the issue of the individual and the social is a paradoxical position. The theory of VC reflects the commitment to the individual as the central figure in the value sphere. According to Kazepides, VC reflects an organismic, individualistic view of human development that sees valuing as ultimately a narcissistic, irrational expression of personal preferences, feelings, and attitudes.[14] That is, on one hand, VC would seem to reflect a notion of morality as essentially a matter of individual expression, determination, and validation. At the same time, the practice of VC seems to imply and result in a process of value resolution or decision making that is significantly affected by group norms and peer pressures. The theory seems to neglect a truth that expresses itself in the practice of VC: children and adults are not islands, and they are easily coerced to respond to value issues in ways that will not embarrass or hurt them in the eyes of their peers. Thus, while VC would purport to be one major contemporary spokesman of the personal approach to valuing, its practice often reflects and preaches a collective, conventional perspective.

MORAL PRINCIPLES

A second cardinal assumption of VC is that at present there is no one conclusive, agreed-upon, definitive body of moral principles or values:

> We do believe that in the world today there is not *one* true religion, one true morality, one true political constitution.[15]

> We cannot give children an absolute set of values, but we can give them something better. We can give them a system that they can use to arrive at their own values.[16]

The claim is that there is no one exclusive body of moral truths that can determine human behavior; hence, there is no one body of moral truths that can be imposed on children. Thus, we should not teach children a bag of values or virtues; instead, we should teach them a "process of valuing."[17]

There are three issues vis à vis VC and moral principles that are relevant to our discussion: (1) Does VC have a notion of *moral* principles? (2) Does VC's approach include a notion of moral principles as an aspect of education? (3) Is VC itself bereft of any substantive moral principles of its own?

The title of this section is "Moral Principles" — yet this is a phrase that does not appear often in VC (and usually only in a critical sense). Instead, VC more characteristically uses the term 'values'. Indeed, this raises the larger question of whether VC is, in fact, as it is usually characterized, about the moral sphere and moral education.

Lockwood, Kazepides, Rokeach, and Stewart point out that VC encompasses a disparate collection of variegated issues under the rubric of values, so that "questions about capital punishment, the legalization of abortion, what toothpaste one prefers, whether God exists, whether one uses mouth wash regularly or whether one likes yogurt are treated as if all were of the same logical type or equally important."[18] Thus, among the topics presented in *Values and Teaching* as appropriate VC topics are: "Pets and You," "TV, Comics, and Violence," "Education for Creativity," "A Student's Report of a Campus Incident" (on cheating), a poem of deviance, "Graduation Day" (blacks and whites at a high school graduation in Americus, Georgia in 1961), and "A List of Alternatives for a Winter Vacation."[19]

VC does not deal with 'morality' or the moral sphere as a distinct sphere of human discourse or activity, but rather, lumps it together with many other issues of personal preference into a category called 'values', which it defines as "general guides to behavior which tend to give direction to life."[20] The word 'value' is used in the broadest sense to refer to personal preferences, inclinations, and choice, and it does not usually distinguish between value issues that are 'moral' as opposed to 'nonmoral' in nature. The analytic point, then, is that VC really does not have a notion of 'moral values' or of moral 'principles' since it does not specifically deal with or delineate the term 'moral'. Both philosophers and educators have claimed that this lack of delineation and sophistication trivializes great moral issues by making them equivalent to the choice of a new dress or an ice-cream cone.[21]

A careful reading of VC literature shows that it has been quite consistent in using the phrase 'values education' rather than 'moral education' to define itself. This point is further emphasized in the revised version of VC as VC$_2$, where the approach is placed in the broader context of humanistic education.[22] VC has consistently stated what its critics charge: it is not a theory or practice of moral education *per se* (with a specifically delineated notion of morality), but rather, it is part of a more general educational approach that is often described as the self-realization and/or humanistic education movement.

We have suggested that VC is not about morality or *moral* principles *per se*. Now the question is whether it is at all about principles, moral or otherwise. VC advocates are skeptical and wary of the notion of principles, which they understand to refer to absolute or authoritative conclusions or prescriptions. They contend that there are no such universally applicable or valid statements in the value domain, and they oppose educational movements that put such statements at the center of their activity.

Kazepides indicates that this position is expressed in VC by the shift in terminology from 'principles' to 'values' and from 'values' to 'valuing'.[23] The new emphasis on 'values' and 'valuing' focuses not on the universality of such statements, but rather, on their personal and experiential qualities:

> Values and valuing are uniquely personal dimensions of the human experience.[24]

> A value indicator is a belief, an opinion, an attitude, an interest, or an isolated act that lets us know that we are in the process of forming a value.[25]

> We have said that values are a product of personal experiences . . . they are not just a matter of true or false. . . . Consequently we are dealing with an area that is not a matter of proof or consensus, but a matter of experience.[26]

> By our definition, and as we see it, by social right, values are personal things.[27]

Thus, VC is based on the notion of a genre of statements that express personal preferences or likes or dislikes and that evolve from the personal experience of the individual. Such statements are assumed to be different than the statements of fact. Moreover, such statements are regarded as personal in the sense that they are rooted in and ultimately determined by the individual and his experience, rather than by social forces or contexts.

VC's stance on values has often been labeled as relativist and emotivist. Critics use the former term to indicate either that VC theorists do not believe in the existence of one definitive set of values that are valid for all human experience or that they do not imply a commitment to normative values as part of the valuing process. The first claim is correct in the sense that VC does deny on epistemological grounds the existence of one conclusive set of values; instead, it argues that values relate to and flow from individual human experience. However, the latter charge, namely, the alleged rejection of values in valuing, is inaccurate. As we shall shortly see, VC clearly affirms the role of values, and indeed, ironically, it presents the most specific list of normative values of any of the approaches under consideration.

The emotivist claim with respect to VC implies that the approach assumes that value statements are exclusively personal statements that express a specific personal emotion (like "oh dear," "I like it!"), rather than constituting some form of evaluative and/or conceptual statement. This charge too would seem to be exaggerated. It is true that VC regards value statements as personal; however, this does not mean that it regards them as personal grunts, groans, or sighs. Indeed, VC seems to treat value statements as very real and relevant expressions that are not necessarily careless or meaningless. "Valuing is a matter of planning, accepting, enhancing, and changing ourselves as individuals, of engaging in the kind of learning which involves our hearts and our souls, as well as our minds."[28] All versions of the valuing process include not only expressive dimensions ("I like," "I feel," "I prefer") but also the dimensions of 'thinking' and 'choosing'. The fact that VC replaces the notion of 'principles' with 'values' in a personal and relativist sense, does not preclude the fact that it also includes normative yet not exclusively emotional statements in the valuing process.

A careful look at the literature of VC reveals the inaccuracy of the charge of its valuelessness. Kirschenbaum argues that VC is not valueless in the sense that it expresses no value preferences. Rather, he argues that there always has been a set of values implicit and explicit in VC that are regarded as "true" and "good": "we value rationality," "we value justice," "we value creativity," "we value autonomy or freedom," and "we value equality."[29] Raths makes the following claim in his new introduction to the second edition of *Values and Teaching*:

> For this we were labelled ethical relativists. In one interpretation, the label is correct; we do believe in the world today there is not *one* true religion, *one* true morality, *one* true political constitution. But a second interpretation does not describe our point of view: we do not believe that any one belief or purpose or attitude is as good as another. We too have preferences; we too have made choices, and while we do not believe that our views are eternal . . . we do believe that they are to be preferred.[30]

Some critics argue that VC is particularly value-laden, to the point of being highly judgmental and as moralistic and preachy as many of the movements it comes to reject.[31] Rokeach claims that VC's alleged value neutrality is misleading: "Values clarification's insistence about value neutrality notwithstanding, an examination of its basic tenets suggests that it nonetheless has certain value commitments that remain silent, and that it moreover attempts through the backdoor to inculcate students with these values."[32] Indeed, of all the approaches to values education that we are examining, VC ironically emerges as the one that either overtly or covertly reveals in the most concrete ways a specific bag of value preferences. It preaches and practices a humanistic ethic of openness, concern for others, self-awareness, and thoughtfulness. Thus, VC differs strikingly from Durkheim and Wilson in regard to social and universal dimensions of the moral principle; it also differs from them in its being the most specifically and practically normative of all the contemporary approaches to values education.

REASON IN ETHICS

The third subcategory of the process of valuing according to VC_1 is choosing:

> *choosing after thoughtful consideration of the consequences of each alternative.* Impulsive or thoughtless choices do not lead to values as we define them. For something to intelligently and meaningfully guide one's life, it must emerge from a weighing and an understanding. Only when the consequences of each of the alternatives are clearly understood can we make intelligent choices. There is an important cognitive factor here. A value can emerge only with thoughtful consideration of the range of the alternatives and the consequences in a choice.[33]

The revised edition of *Values and Teaching* extends the discussion of reason and valuing even further by including a new chapter on "Values and Thinking," in which ten categories of thinking are related to valuing (comparing, classifying, observing and reporting, summarizing, interpreting, analyzing assumptions, problem solving, criticizing and evaluating, imagining and creating, coding and reactions to coding).[34] VC_2 takes VC_1's original category of 'choosing' and divides it into two separate categories: 'thinking' and 'choosing', with the former encompassing four subcategories (thinking on various levels, critical thinking, moral reasoning on the higher levels, and divergent or creative thinking) and the latter including two subcategories (considering consequences and achievement planning). Thus,

VC₂'s revisions on this score come to emphasize and make more specific the role of reasoning in valuing.

At the same time, VC uses the notion of reasoning or thinking in the values domain in a telegraphic and undeveloped way. It does not conceptually elaborate a theory of reasoning and/or thinking in ethics. VC spokespeople have suggested that such theorists as Dewey, Kohlberg, Raths, and Bloom reflect the VC conception of cognition and valuing;[35] however, this list is too disparate and broad to be helpful in the explication of VC on this topic.

Thus, beyond the claim that thinking is a dimension of the valuing process and a specification of some dimensions of such thinking, the theoretical literature of VC is not particularly helpful in elucidating this point. At the same time, there are other themes and emphases in the theory and practice of VC that have led some to regard it as a prominent contemporary approach to values education that *de-emphasizes* the role of reason in valuing.

First, revisionist VC₂ theorists themselves argued that VC₁ was too cognitive. VC₂ spokespeople called instead for an increased emphasis on the deepening of the awareness of the individual's own feelings.[36] Second, the practice of VC as expressed in its exercises reveals a de-emphasis on the reasoning components of the valuing process, as compared with the prizing or choosing components. A quantitative analysis of the exercises in *Values and Teaching* reveals that the majority of the exercises are in the acting and prizing categories, while a minority is concerned with the choosing domain.

This impression is strengthened by the nature of the questions and interactive style proposed by VC. Teachers are urged to use brief, evocative questions and comments; they are not (with the exception of Chapter 10 in the revised edition of *Values and Teaching*) presented with models of lengthy, involved dialogues, but with lists of short, trigger-type questions. Moreover, teachers are not encouraged to engage in lengthy follow-ups to student responses, but to end discussions quickly and even abruptly. Indeed, one of the dominant pedagogic thrusts of VC is toward the short, evocative statement, rather than the elongated, elaborated discursive interchange.

This style has led some critics to argue that VC's notion of 'clarification' is less demanding, less critical, and less evaluative than the notions of moral deliberation and thinking; moreover, it ultimately reflects VC's main thrusts, such as the candid confrontation with and expression of personal feelings.[37] According to this reading of VC, its essential conception of reasoning is as reflection on and expression of personal feelings and preferences. It is, then, neither a social nor an objectivist notion of reason and values, but rather, a personalist-expressionist theory.

Once again, we are left with a paradoxical dualism in VC. Its brief theoretical statements propose to align it with some aspect of the cognitive school of ethics, but its much more sustained practical literature seems to transform it into a prime representative of a neononcognitive notion of morality. The child who would most likely emerge from the VC process of education for valuing is likely to be more proficient at personal expression than at moral reasoning.

FORM AND CONTENT

Values clarification is supposedly the exemplar of the notion that the process of valuing, rather than specific contents called values, constitutes the heart of values education. According to this position, values education is about the development of the valuing process in children, not the transmission of specific value contents. VC spokespeople admit that there is some distinction between 'value' and 'valuing'; however, their ultimate concern is with the assimilation of the former into the latter: "We cannot give children an absolute set of values, but we can give them something better. We can give them a system that they can use to arrive at their own values."[38]

There are two primary reasons for VC spokespeople's preoccupation with valuing rather than values: (1) as already seen, its adherents believe that values are in flux, and any specific values that we may teach today might be irrelevant tomorrow, and (2) they believe that it can provide a more lasting and functional legacy to children, that is, a technique that will enable them to solve their own value dilemmas.

VC adherents' emphasis on the teaching of a process is influenced by two disparate models. The first is the therapeutic model of the student as client who is to be helped by the therapist to develop his/her own tools and abilities to deal with a host of events that will occur. The second is the disciplinary model of the child as a young historian, scientist, or philosopher (as expounded in some of the major curriculum projects of the 1960s); the assumption is that we should not teach the child all the "facts" of history, science, or philosophy, but rather how to think historically, scientifically, or philosophically.

Thus, VC spokespeople claim that it is about the teaching of a process; is this claim, in fact, accurate? The notion of a process that VC adherents would like to emulate is in the sense of a series of nonnormative skills, which when combined together would comprise the process. Education in such a process would involve presenting such skills to the young and training and monitoring their ability to perform them. For example, if the process to be taught is running, then the necessary skills would include: stretching, breathing in a certain way, moving the hands in a certain pattern, and controlling the lungs in certain ways. VC theorists would want to believe that the process of valuing is comprised of a series of skills in the same sense that swimming, running, and riding a bicycle are (realizing, of course, that the contents and sequences of skills in each of these areas are not the same).

Are the skills of VC — choosing, prizing, acting, thinking, and communicating — of the same order as the skills of running or swimming? We have seen from our discussions of thinking and ethics in Durkheim and Wilson that thinking, in fact, is not an agreed upon skill area; it means many different things and assumes different forms, depending upon the basic epistemological assumptions of the systems. Similarly, the skills of choosing or communicating in VC are activities that presuppose some basic value stances. The point is that the skills of VC are forms or reflections of value statements. The process of valuing as enunciated by VC is different from other processes such as swimming, running, and thinking philosophically, in that it already requires and reflects the acceptance of a host of values with respect to rationality, justice, autonomy, and communication. The process of VC is, ultimately, a philosophy of values.

There are those who support the VC theorists' claim that it is essentially about a process; however, they suggest that the VC process is closer to models of client-centered therapy or self-realization, than to models of moral deliberation or reflecton. According to this claim, VC is really about the skills and abilities necessary for the individual to confront his/her feelings and thoughts and to feel competent and comfortable with them and with other people. Thus, VC, it is argued, is mainly about a person's ability to relate to him/herself. However, this type of activity is different from the normal sense of the notion of moral education, which usually is understood as at least minimally involving some sort of confrontation between the individual and a set of moral standards or stances.[39] The claim, therefore, is that VC is actually about a process that, while related to the moral and/or values domain, is ultimately of a different sort, genre, or focus.

Thus, VC's radical stance on the exclusiveness of its concern with process proves to be more problematic and complicated than would seem to be the case at first glance. At the same time, VC (considered together with Wilson) clearly constitutes one of the prominent new approaches to moral education that claims to place a process rather than specific contents at the center of the moral education enterprise.

ACTION

Action or acting appear as constituent components of every formulation of VC. In VC_1, 'acting' was characterized by two dimensions: (1) doing something with choices the individual has made and (2) doing something repeatedly in some pattern of life.[40] This category was expanded by Kirschenbaum to include acting repeatedly, acting consistently, and acting skillfully.[41] All versions of VC emphasize that all the criteria of valuing, including acting, are crucial in order for something to become a value; otherwise, it remains a belief or an attitude.

There are two prominent characteristics of acting in VC. First, action is expected to be related to and flow from the previous dimensions of valuing, that is, from thinking, choosing, and prizing. Actions are thus not regarded as isolated nor spontaneous phenomena; rather, they should be outgrowths and expressions of considerations and choices that an individual has freely chosen. The link between actions in the values sphere and other elements of valuing is central for VC, and VC is one of the prominent spokesmen of the inherent and indispensable link between thought, motivation, and action in a life of value.

The second aspect of action in the value sphere according to VC is the notion of pattern. Valuing, according to VC, implies a systematic repetition of actions, rather than a momentary, idiosyncratic performance. Actions become a genuine dimension of the valuing process when they are organized in a series of repeatable, consistent patterns.

VC's emphasis on the integration of thought, motivation, and action aligns it with some major classical and contemporary moral theories that have emphasized the important link between a person's reasons and intentions and the consequent deeds. It also distinguishes VC from notions of morality in which the actions *per se* are regarded as the prominent defining factors. Morality for VC is not only a system of actions but also one in which actions flow from other, very personal sources.

The stance of VC vis à vis the notion of moral or value habits is a somewhat complicated matter. On one hand, it clearly proposes to be a corrective for an exclusively habitual notion of morality as a system of actions imposed on a person from without. At the same time, the notion of habit does surface in several aspects of VC. First, many of the VC activities are based on the assumption that young people already have engaged in and reflected on various forms of values activities and habits. Students are asked to reflect upon deeds they have done and habits they have: "How did you feel when that happened?" "Did you consider any alternatives?" "Do you do this often?" "Would you do the same things again?"[42] These questions assume that already performed values, deeds, and habits are a part of a person's life. Hence, VC is not a simplistic motivational theory of moral action that assumes that the movement in the values domain is always from reflection→intention→ action. It would also seem to assume the existence of habit as a reality of the values domain, and to be concerned with infusing habit with reflection and intention: habit→intention→reflection.

The reality of habit as a dimension of the values domain also surfaces in the previously discussed notion of repetition and pattern. VC does not seem to be claiming that every values decision is the outcome of a complex personal confrontation with a dilemma; instead, it implies that actions should eventually fall into recognizable patterns or repetitive constructs such that certain sorts of situations will result in certain sorts of actions. The notion of habit in VC is admittedly underdeveloped, and we are only able to approach it by implication from its practical literature. At the same time, the notion does seem to exist and be a factor in the life of the valuing person.

The two major criticisms of VC that have been voiced concerning the action component are that (1) acting is ultimately the least emphasized of the valuing components and (2) VC trivializes acting by not clearly distinguishing between value and nonvalue actions. The analysis of the vast pedagogic literature of VC reveals that the major pedagogical focus of VC has been on the development of choosing and prizing. VC generally and VC_2 particularly seem to be concerned with the ability to reflect on and have feelings toward choices and deeds, rather than with the ability to perform deeds. While VC does not imply that actions are irrelevant, it does not devote the same pedagogic effort to helping children learn how to perform value actions. It neglects what Frankena calls MEY (Moral Education Y), the teaching of how to perform moral deeds. Many philosophers and educators have agreed that children also need training in how to carry out moral or value actions; this is not something that comes easily or automatically or for which there are enough accessible models today. Such a type of exercise or training is deemphasized in VC.

The second problem is VC's trivialization of the action sphere. For example, in discussing the plateau of "acting according to one's beliefs," Simon and Olds present the example of where someone should park his/her car in the shopping center parking lot.[43] Other examples of acting in the values sphere in VC are what clothes to wear, what route to take, what flavor ice cream to eat.[44] The problem with VC in this instance is that it simply has not distinguished between value or moral actions and other kinds of actions. Where to park or what flavor ice cream to eat are questions of which action to choose, but they surely are different in nature than the question of whether to support one's aged parents, fight for the Free

French, or protest against a war or not. A person is confronted with a host of alternative actions in life; they are all not of the same sort in the sense that all are derived in the same way or that all are of the same order. To treat all actions as if they were the same is not only to trivialize some actions and to inflate others but also to inadequately prepare a person to act. The way we handle alternative choices, for example, which sweater to buy or which flavor ice cream to eat, differs radically from choice to choice, and an education that does not distinguish between these choices severely limits the range of actions of a person.

THE MORALLY EDUCATED PERSON

Who is the "morally educated person" according to VC? The notion is in itself somewhat uncharacteristic because, as we have already noted, VC is not exclusively aimed at the moral sphere and because it is ultimately probably more concerned with the "healthy" person than the "educated" person. Nevertheless, it is possible to talk about the person who is the desired outcome in the VC approach: such a person is one who has developed the ability to use several different skills that constitute 'valuing'. These skills encompass cognitive, affective, self-reflective, and behavioral abilities. The valuing person is one who becomes equipped to become the "locus of evaluation" for his/herself.

In one sense, the morally educated person is a technocrat, or one who has mastered a body of instrumental skills or abilities. The valuing subprocesses do not, at least overtly, propose to reflect a moral point of view, moral conscience, or the disposition to be moral. Instead, they entail the ability to acquire and apply a series of skills that constitute valuing. Thus, ironically, the "morally educated person" of VC is a "trained person" who has become proficient at implementing certain skills.

The social context is, according to VC, an arena in which value issues often occur; however, it is merely a setting rather than an integral factor in the valuing process. The valuing process may take place in social contexts and may relate to social issues, but it is not informed by the social domain. To be morally educated according to VC standards does not require dependence on a link with any great cultural or moral tradition or body of values. To the extent that great traditions could be programatically valuable in stimulating the valuing process, they are valuable; however, great traditions carry no authority *per se*, and the systematic study of Christianity, Judaism, humanism, and socialism are not indispensable to the VC approach.

Ultimately, the morally educated person in VC is the educated person and the educated person is one who has a healthy sense of self and relationship with others. Once again, it would seem that VC is, in fact, much less about morality or education and much more about the person.

INDOCTRINATION

The writings of VC refer often to the term 'indoctrination' and it is one of the unpopular concepts of the lexicon. Indeed, one of the very reasons for VC's genesis was the concern with rejecting indoctrination as a legitimate educational concept and activity. However, while VC uses the term 'indoctrination' often, it rarely defines it; instead 'indoctrination' has the red flag function in this literature of referring to a host of activities often associated with education that VC regards as undesirable. The negative phrase 'indoctrinaton' is contrasted in this approach by the positive (green flag) phrase 'values clarification'.[45]

In this literature, indoctrination is associated with such (negative) words as "inculcating," "instilling," "fostering,"[46] "moralizing," "imposition," and "brainwashing."[47] Generally, there seem to be three qualities that characterize the wide range of activities included in 'indoctrination' according to VC.

First, 'indoctrination' is based on the (faulty) premise that educators know "the right set of values" that they are entitled to pass on to children. The quality that is unacceptable in this instance is the notion of conclusiveness, that is, the assumption that there are verified, agreed-upon, and definitive answers to value questions. The starting point of VC is, in fact, the assumption that the world is constantly changing and that there are today no conclusive or verified answers to value questions. Hence, 'indoctrination' is characterized by overambitious epistemological assumptions.

However, 'indoctrination' according to VC also implies a certain teaching process ("the indoctrinary procedures of the past fail to help people grapple with all the confusion and conflict of today").[48] In this case, the objection is to styles of education that 'transfer', 'transmit', and 'manipulate'. The verbs that are preferred to describe (values) education are 'examine', 'clarify', 'arrive at', 'consider'.[49] Thus, 'indoctrination' here clearly implies a series of methods that are very teacher centered, that treat the child as a passive and malleable agent, and that come to shape and form.

The third aspect of 'indoctrination' that surfaces in this literature is depersonalization. 'Indoctrination' implies recognition of the legitimacy of the past, heroes, and history as legitimizing forces; in so doing, according to VC, 'indoctrination' minimizes the individual. 'Indoctrination' establishes people, places, and ideologies as desirable or significant models of influence, and in this way overwhelms children and extinguishes or seriously impedes their own deliberation and choice. Thus, the problem with 'indoctrination' is not just that it is rooted in what it thinks are the right answers or that it is heavy handed; it is also too impersonal and other-directed rather than inner-directed.

VC's discussion of 'indoctrination' is striking on two counts. First, this term is certainly the "enemy," and it is attacked and rejected on every VC front. In that sense, VC is very much a contemporary approach to values education defined and obsessed by the notion of 'indoctrination'. Second, VC is strikingly careless and nonanalytic in its treatment of the concept. We know that there is an enemy, and we are presented with many words or garments that are associated with the enemy; but we are never precisely told who we should be against or why. In this case, a clarification approach opts for ambiguity rather than clarity.

THE ROLE OF THE TEACHER

The teacher's role is clearly defined in VC as the orchestrator of learning situations that will enable the development of the basic valuing sub-processes. The VC teacher does not come to teach specific substantive values or to be a role model for desired moral behavior, but rather to be a technician who facilitates the development of a series of technical skills.

This means that the teacher's own values, behavior, and personal life-style are not directly relevant to his/her teaching activity; indeed, VC argues for the neutrality of the teacher in terms of the place of his/her own values in the teaching activity. This notion of neutrality does not mean that the teacher should not maintain or even express his/her own values; rather, it means that the personal values held by the teacher should not interfere with the more basic function of developing the valuing process.

Hence, the teacher of VC is viewed neither as a representative of society as in Durkheim, or as a model of advanced value stages as in Kohlberg, or as a formal teacher of a moral philosophic style as in Wilson. Rather, the teacher in VC is close to the model of therapist or facilitator[50] who, via appropriate questions and nudges, helps the client to develop and draw upon his/her own abilities. Indeed, some of the prominent traits prescribed by VC for the teacher resemble the role of the therapist in certain forms of psychotherapy: the brevity of his/her intervention, the clearly defined time parameters, the sharp separation of therapist's own values and those of the patient, the lack of reference to an external body of values as a potential source of insight.

As we noted at the beginning of this chapter, VC has proven to be very popular with teachers, and that reality is one educators should take serious-ly. The many pluses of VC seem to be that (1) it can be learned quickly, (2) opportunities to learn VC are readily available and at a reasonable time and financial investment, (3) it is applicable to a host of classroom and subject areas, and it is not relevant only to a limited number of subjects, (4) it apparently arouses interest and involvement of students, and (5) it does not demand of the teacher rigorous confrontation with and mastery of complex philosophical or psychological issues, nor does it require the teacher to formulate or accept a specific philosophic system. Instead, in effect it tells the teacher that he or she can engage in values education in a multitude of areas within the context of the school life and from whatever the teacher's own value perspective may be at the moment.

VC does not denigrate or deemphasize the role of the teacher in values education. Instead, it shifts the emphasis from the teacher as source or representative of moral truth, or from the teacher as model of moral deliber-ation, to the teacher as trainer-therapist who, via the proper questioning procedure, helps the individual to develop the skills necessary to become a valuing person.

PEDAGOGY

In an exchange with Lawrence Kohlberg on the virtues and problems of his approach as compared with VC, Sidney Simon indicated that Kohlberg is for researchers and VC is for teachers.[51] In an uncharacteristically, un-VC-like nonresponse to John Stewart's discussion of "Problems and Contradictions of Values Clarification," Simon distinguishes between those who are concerned with research ("Stewart's real interest seems to be with dazzling his academic, ivory tower peer group") and those concerned with educational practice ("I don't think he is really concerned with making this life better for teachers and children").[52] While there might be disagreement as to whether VC's practical focus is simply "a set of cute but superficial games or gimmicks"[53] or, in fact, constitutes a full-blown theory of educa-tion, there would be little disagreement that its domain and impact is very centrally located in the world of practice. The thousands of copies of books on VC that have been sold are mostly compendia of methods, approaches, and classroom activities for teachers.

This vast practical literature delineates three main categories of strate-gies. The first is a dialogue strategy and refers to a style of response ("the clarifying response"), which the teachers are trained to use to facilitate the valuing process. This response has ten qualities:[54]

1. It avoids moralizing, criticizing, giving values, or evaluating.
2. It puts responsibility on the students to consider their own ideas and behaviors.
3. It is persuasive and stimulating, but not insistent; it enables the student to decline to participate if he/she so desires.
4. "It does not try to do big things with its small contents"; it aims at setting a mood and at stimulating thought.
5. It is not used to obtain data or for interview purposes.
6. It usually is not characterized by extended discussion; indeed, it often cuts discussion off at a certain point.
7. Clarifying responses are often for individuals; values are personal things and teachers often use clarifying responses to relate to specific individuals.
8. It need not be used to respond to everything everyone says or does in a classroom.
9. "Clarifying responses operate in situations where there are no "right answers."
10. They are not mechanical formulae.

The dialogue strategy, then, is a form of question and answer style that causes the student to use the essential valuing processes.

Second, there are a host of writing activities that VC adherents propose that are concerned with the same tasks as the dialogue strategy and the clarifying response, except that it is in written form and it focuses more on group discussion. One of the characteristic forms of the writing strategy is the value sheet, which is a provocative statement and a series of questions passed out to students and later discussed by the group:

Value Sheet 1
The Meditation Room at the U.N.

Directions: Please answer as many of the questions below as you wish, but answer them thoughtfully and honestly. I will collect the papers at the end of the study period and return them to you with occasional comments later in the week. This is an optional assignment and has no effect on grades, of course.

There is a chapel or meditation room at the U.N. General Assembly building in New York that has had all symbols of particular religions removed. There is nothing there but some rows of chairs, a potted plant, and a shaft of light. Marya Mannes writes of this room:

"It seemed to me standing there that this nothingness was so oppressive and disturbing that it became a sort of madness, and the room a sort of padded cell. It seemed to me that the core of our greatest contemporary trouble lay here, that all this whiteness and shapelessness and weakness was the leukemia of noncommitment, sapping our strength. We had found, finally, that only nothing could please all, and we were trying to make the greatest of all generalities out of that most singular truth, the spirit of man. The terrifying thing about this room was that it made no statement whatever. In its capacity and constriction, it could not even act as a reflector of thought" [From M. Mannes, "Meditations in an Empty Room," *The Reporter*, Feb. 23, 1956; republished in M. Ascoli (ed.), *Our Times: The Best from The Reporter Magazine* (New York: Farrar, Straus & Giroux, Inc., 1960)].

1. Write your reaction to this quotation in just a few words.

2. What emotions does it produce?

3. Are there some reasons for believing that Mannes' quotation is "anti-religious"? If not, why? If yes, in which ways?

4. In your mind, does Mannes, in the quotation above, exaggerate the danger which she sees? Explain.

5. Can you list some more examples in our society which tend to support Mannes' point?

6. Can you list any which tend to refute her point of view?

7. If this quotation suggests a problem which worries you, are there some things you might personally do about it? Within yourself? With some close friends? With the larger society?

8. Is there any wisdom from the past which you can cite to ease Mannes' concern? is there any wisdom from the past which might alarm her even more?

9. What do you get aroused about? Are you doing anything about it?[55]

Values sheets can encompass all sorts of topics and subject areas, including science, foreign languages, mathematics, history, current events, and social problems. Indeed, VC emphasizes that its methods are appropriate for a broad range of subject areas, and it does not conceive of itself as operating solely within the confines of an area narrowly defined as "value education."

A third group of activities focuses directly on group discussion and group process. Such activities are concerned with utilizing the group to help individuals focus more carefully on their own personal reactions to value issues. Such activities include pictures without captions, scenes from plays or movies, provocative questions, and humorous stories. These activities are used in various ways in the class group or in small subunits. The thrust of this category is to utilize the group experience as a vehicle to self-education in valuing.

The various books of VC list hundreds of activities that generally fall into these three categories. In addition, lengthy lists of specific questions that usually correspond to specific subvaluing processes are offered (for example, a teacher is presented with a list of questions aimed at stimulating choosing, prizing, acting, and their respective subcategories).

Finally, there are specialized volumes concerned with the application of VC to specific groups and needs, for example, exceptional children;[56] parents;[57] counselors;[58] and religious education.[59] Such volumes attempt to apply the general principles and assumptions of VC to specific locales, populations, and needs, and they too usually devote the bulk of their pages to practical examples from the specific context.

Thus, pedagogy is the domain that has been the main concern of VC, and it is the area that has generated the greatest number of pages. The basic assumptions of VC's pedagogy are that it should promote accessible and easily replicable pedagogic examples; it should present styles and techniques aimed at a broad range of curricular and cocurricular areas of the school, rather than being restricted to one subject *per se* called moral or values education; its thrust is technical, aimed at the development of a series of skills and abilities essential to functioning as a valuing person.

VC does not overtly deal with the development of a learning theory for values education. Its critics have argued that it has no theoretical base; its proponents argue that "it in fact includes an important set of attitudes and hypotheses about the nature of human growth and development."[60] Indeed, Kirschenbaum claims that VC is supported by a significant base of psychological theory and research from such diverse areas as moral reasoning, critical thinking, creativity and problem solving, self-concept, psychotherapy, achievement motivation, and group dynamics.[61] The fact is, however, that nowhere is there a full-blown presentation of a theory of how children learn and at best we can only point to some directions that seem implicit in VC.

First, the three or five or seven or more subprocesses of VC are not presented as developmental stages. (In that sense, they are closer to Wilson's moral components than to Kohlberg's stages of moral development.) VC does not claim that the individual has to pursue these subprocesses in the order that they are listed or that the order is hierarchical.

Second, VC allows for the fact that someone might not engage in all seven subprocesses; that is, some people might choose or prize, but not act or vice versa. Such a development is characterized by the distinction made between 'values' (preferences that are the result of the application of all seven processes), and 'beliefs', 'attitudes', or 'value indicators', (positions or stances that do not satisfy all seven of the subprocesses).

The status of the seven "processes" has always been somewhat unclear in VC and is the subject of internal disagreement. In VC_1, the seven processes are described as 'criteria', which would seem to mean seven standards or requirements that a person must utilize in order to be referred to as a 'valuing person' and that must be implemented in order for a belief to become a value. VC_2 theorists, however, are unhappy with the notion of 'criteria' for two reasons. First, they note that these criteria are not always specific or functional enough. For example, the original statement of the seven subprocesses does not indicate how proud someone must be or how many times he/she must publicly affirm something in order to fulfill the prizing criterion; also it does not delineate precisely enough how many consequences someone must consider or how free someone must be in order to fulfill the choosing criterion. The second reservation of VC₂ vis à vis the notion of criteria is that it is too rigid, external, and fixed. The goal is not for people to fulfill seven externally set criteria:

> Therefore, I prefer to talk only of the *processes* of valuing, to emphasize that there are seven ways we develop and enrich the values in our lives — by getting in touch with what we prize and cherish, by considering alternatives, by acting on our beliefs and goals, by examining our patterns, and so on. My goal is not for people to be able to say, "Look here, I've got five values which meet all seven criteria," but to help people, including myself, learn to use skillfully the seven processes in our lives. Then, as a matter of course, we will continue to examine what we prize and cherish, make thoughtful choices from alternatives, act on our beliefs and goals — *but only when we feel the need to do so and not just to meet someone else's criteria.* It seems to me that one of the overall goals of values clarification is to return the locus of evaluation to the person, so that he is the controller of his own valuing process. The seven criteria imply an external frame of reference which seems inimical to values clarification. I want to use the seven valuing processes in my life because they help my inner needs find expression and fulfillment. I do not want to use them because they are criteria.[62]

These are the explicit aspects of learning in VC; what are some of the implicit elements? Kazepides summarizes some implicit epistemological assumptions of VC. First, it assumes an individualistic learning model in the sense that children's learning is regarded as taking place with little relationship to historical, social, or philosophical contexts. VC's emphasis on returning the locus of evaluation to its proper address, that is, the individual, reflects, in fact, a narcissistic model of learning. Second, despite its avowed commitment to reasoning, Kazepides and others claim that VC is ultimately "a betrayal of reason and a retreat into irrationalism."[63] The great emphasis on the personal and the individual, and the concomitant deemphasis of the public, the collective, the linguistic, turn reflection into an essentially private and even mystical experience. VC often seems to be suggesting that learning and knowing imply the ability to be in touch with and express one's self. This emphasis on the expression of self, whatever that may entail, has led some to argue that VC (especially VC₂) is, in fact, an ultimately deterministic conception that attributes great power to senses and feelings and much less to the agent's conscious, considered interventions.

Some of these criticisms probably exaggerate what were the genuine intentions of VC. At the same time, they point to the problems of a system of values education that has not related to a host of issues relevant to its own sphere. The result is often that unintentional misrepresentations or results occur, both in theory and more seriously in practice. Indeed, the critics of VC frequently claim that the incompleteness of VC as a theory of values education may lead to results that are exactly the opposite from those intended.

SUMMARY

The academic world has generally not treated VC with the respect that it shows toward Durkheim or Kohlberg or Dewey. Yet there is a sense in which VC is of much greater significance and import than the theories of these three men or many other approaches to moral education in the twentieth century. VC's importance lies in the fact that it is a symbolic barometer of the frustration and the hope of the world of education vis à vis the values domain. VC is a particularly strong statement of the values flux of contemporary society, the dissatisfaction with approaches to values education used by schools in the past, and the belief that values education is an honorable and crucial function of schools. Moreover, it highlights the fact that the crucial arena for any approach to values education is the classroom, the child, and the teacher. Indeed, it challenges theory with the contention that the only true test of an approach to values education is in the domain of practice. In that sense, it certainly is perhaps the most paradigmatic of contemporary values education approaches.

Chapter 5

LAWRENCE KOHLBERG: THE COGNITIVE-DEVELOPMENTAL APPROACH TO MORAL EDUCATION

THE MOST PROMINENT NAME in the contemporary renaissance of moral education is Lawrence Kohlberg. Kohlberg's work dominates the discussion of moral education in the university world, learned and popular journals, and symposia and seminars. He is known to philosophers and principals, psychologists and prison wardens, sociologists and school teachers. There are few discussions of moral education today at academic conferences or at informal gatherings in which the name of Lawrence Kohlberg does not appear.

It has been suggested that the Kohlberg bandwagon ultimately reflects the search of late twentieth-century American education and psychology for a definitive value gospel and faith as a response to the values relativism and malaise of mid-century America.[1] Kohlberg cannot only be seen in this light; the great interest in him is clearly also related to the scope and magnitude of the enterprise which he has undertaken. He is singular among recent theorists of moral education in his quest for a synthesis of the spheres of philosophy, psychology, sociology, and education into an integrated theory and practice of moral education. Philosophically, Kohlberg's work represents a reaction to the analytic direction of much of twentieth-century educational philosophy, and a return to the grand tradition of a synthetic philosophy of education. Psychologically, he attempts to replace the alleged control of moral education by the Freudians and Skinnerians with an alternative psychological basis.[2] Sociologically, Kohlberg proposes a new universalism in response to the moral relativism of the modern age. Educationally, he presents a practice of moral education that teachers can understand and implement. Thus, Kohlberg promises much to an age and educational system that are searching for great answers to great questions; it is no wonder that he is treated so seriously by so many people.

The analysis of Kohlberg's approach is facilitated by the existence of

68

an extensive literature that he and his colleagues have produced.[3] Kohlberg is an accomplished writer, and he has published his views in a diverse array of sources. In addition, he is a dynamic thinker who has not been afraid to hypothesize, review, reexamine, and revise. The early Kohlberg differs from the later Kohlberg on some key issues, and the most recent Kohlberg has readjusted some original assumptions and still leaves some issues unanswered. This extensive literature has previously been available in a series of separate journal articles and monographs; recently, Kohlberg's major writings have been prepared for publication in a three volume series.[4] (We shall draw upon these particular papers in this chapter.)

In addition, there also exists an extensive, second-order, expository literature *on* Kohlberg. Sometimes this literature helps the student better understand and master the master; sometimes it is read and studied *instead* of the master. Not infrequently, the disciples or interpreters of Kohlberg have sometimes *become* the Kohlbergian theory. A pecularity of Kohlberg's work is the extensive set of categories, titles, and labels that have been attached to his theories. These theories have, alternatively, been denoted as structuralism,[5] the cognitive-developmental theory of moral development,[6] progressive interactionism,[7] and constructivism.[8] Similarly, Kohlberg regards his theories as influenced by (among others) Socrates, Kant, Rawls, Dewey, and Piaget. These categorical and historical labels sometimes help to elucidate by referring the student to already recognizable concepts. Sometimes, however, they confuse because the categories themselves are not obvious and/or because it is not always clear which aspects of Kohlberg are being denoted as Kantian, Deweyian, or Piagetian. Moreover, while Socrates, Kant, Dewey, Piaget, and Rawls sometimes get along with each other very well, at other times they prove to be odd bedfellows.

Thus, the richness of Kohlberg has led to the existence of a surrounding army of translators, supporters, and intermediaries who sometimes explicate and sometimes complicate. In our analysis, we shall attempt to relate as much as possible to the original Kohlbergian texts and arguments, and generally we shall try to avoid categories or personal labels that demand lengthy analysis.

INDIVIDUAL AND SOCIAL

Kohlberg's position on the relationship of individual and society in the moral sphere would seem to be definitively described by what he calls his Deweyian interactionism. In fact, this interactionism clearly is one prominent motif in Kohlberg's treatment of this topic; at the same time there occasionally surfaces a surprising ethical individualism in Kohlberg's writings which must be examined and contrasted with his interactionism.

In "Development as the Aim of Education: the Dewey View," Kohlberg delineates three great theories of education, knowledge, and development: romanticism (Rousseau, Freud, Mill), cultural transmission (Durkheim), and progressivism (Dewey).[9] Each theory has its own unique ontological, moral, social, and psychological assumptions and implications. Kohlberg rejects the radical individualism of the romanticist and the radical collectivism of the cultural transmission school, arguing instead for a theory of development based on the notion of a mutual interrelationship between the organism (the person) and the environment:

> The maturationist theory assumes that basic mental structure results from an innate patterning. The environmentalist learning theory assumes that basic mental structure results from the patterning or association of events in the outside world. The cognitive-developmental theory assumes that basic mental structure results from an interaction between organismic structuring tendencies and the structure of the outside world, not reflecting either one directly.[10]

Epistemologically, Kohlberg's position implies a rejection of the notion that knowledge is either essentially an innate experience of self or of a culture. Rather, meaning and truth emerge as dependent on the person's relationship to a situation and a setting. Thus, Kohlberg argues for an integrated notion of morality rooted in the interrelationship of the individual and the society; indeed, he accepts Dewey's contention that the very distinction between the two is meaningless. This inherent link between the individual and the social in morality is underscored in the central role ascribed to the value of justice in Kohlberg's system. Justice as concern for others means that individual human existence is inextricably linked to social contexts; the concern for others is neither a symbol, psychological mechanism, nor cultural artifact; it is rather a basic defining characteristic of the human moral situation. To be human and moral is to interrelate with other people in a social context.

Kohlberg has progressively come to place increasing emphasis on the social nature of morality (and, on his own admission, to move closer to a Durkheimian theory of moral education).[11] This movement is reflected in the reworkings of his original, six-stage taxonomy and in the increased emphasis on the development of a Stage 4 social morality.[12] (See Figure 1 and Figure 2 for the early and later versions of Kohlberg's stages of moral judgment.) This recent thrust may be seen as a response to what some have regarded as an excessive individualism in early Kohlberg.[13] However, the literature reveals that the social theme in its interactionist formulation has been a constant leitmotif of Kohlberg throughout.

(continued on page 75)

FIGURE 1.   Classification of Moral Judgment into Levels and Stages of Development [early version]

LEVELS	BASIS OF MORAL JUDGMENT	STAGES OF DEVELOPMENT
I	Moral value resides in external, quasi-physical happenings, in bad acts, or in quasi-physical needs rather than in persons and standards.	*Stage 1:* Obedience and punishment orientation. Egocentric deference to superior power or prestige, or a trouble-avoiding set. Objective responsibility.
		Stage 2: Naively egoistic orientation. Right action is that instrumentally satisfying the self's needs and occasionally others'. Awareness of relativism of value to each actor's needs and perspective. Naive egalitarianism and orientation to exchange and reciprocity.
II	Moral value resides in performing good or right roles, in maintaining the conventional order and the expectancies of others.	*Stage 3:* Good-boy orientation. Orientation to approval and to pleasing and helping others. Conformity to stereotypical images of majority or natural role behavior, and judgment by intentions.
		Stage 4: Authority and social-order maintaining orientation. Orientation to "doing duty" and to showing respect for authority and maintaining the given social order for its own sake. Regard for earned expectations of others.
III	Moral value resides in conformity by the self to shared or shareable standards, rights, or duties.	*Stage 5:* Contractual legalistic orientation. Recognition of an arbitrary element or starting point in rules or expectations for the sake of agreement. Duty defined in terms of contract, general avoidance of violation of the will or rights of others, and majority will and welfare.
		Stage 6: Conscience or principle orientation. Orientation not only to actually ordained social rules but to principles of choice involving appeal to logical universality and consistency. Orientation to conscience as a directing agent and to mutual respect and trust.

Note: From Lawrence Kohlberg, "Stage and Sequence: The Cognitive-Developmental Approach to Socialization" in HANDBOOK OF SOCIALIZATION THEORY AND RESEARCH, David A. Goslin, Editor. Copyright © 1969 by Houghton Mifflin Company. Used with permission.

FIGURE 2. The Six Stages of Moral Judgment [later version]

LEVEL A. PRECONVENTIONAL LEVEL

STAGE 1.   The Stage of Punishment and Obedience

Content. Right is literal obedience to rules and authority, avoiding punishment, and not doing physical harm.
1. What is right is to avoid breaking rules, to obey for obedience's sake, and to avoid doing physical damage to people and property.
2. The reasons for doing right are avoidance of punishment and the superior power of authorities.

Social Perspective. This stage takes an egocentric point of view. A person at this stage doesn't consider the interests of others or recognize they differ from actor's, and doesn't relate two points of view. Actions are judged in terms of physical consequences rather than in terms of psychological interests of others. Authority's perspective is confused with one's own.

STAGE 2.   The Stage of Individual Instrumental Purpose and Exchange.

Content. Right is serving one's own or other's needs and making fair deals in terms of concrete exchange.
1. What is right is following rules when it is to someone's immediate interest. Right is acting to meet one's own interests and needs and letting others do the same. Right is also what is fair; that is, what is an equal exchange, a deal, an agreement.
2. The reason for doing right is to serve one's own needs or interests in a world where one must recognize that other people have their interests, too.

Social Perspective. This stage takes a concrete individualistic perspective. A person at this stage separates own interests and points of view from those of authorities and others. He or she is aware everybody has individual interests to pursue and these conflict, so that right is relative (in the concrete individualistic sense). The person integrates or relates conflicting individual interests to one another through instrumental exchange of services, through instrumental need for the other and the other's goodwill, or through fairness giving each person the same amount.

LEVEL B. CONVENTIONAL LEVEL

STAGE 3.   The Stage of Mutual Interpersonal Expectations, Relationships, and Conformity

Content. The right is playing a good (nice) role, being concerned about other people and their feelings, keeping loyalty and trust with partners, and being motivated to follow rules and expectations.
1. What is right is living up to what is expected by people close to one or what people generally expect of people in one's role as son, sister, friend, and so on. "Being good" is important and means having good motives, showing concern about others. It also means keeping mutual relationships, maintaining trust, loyalty, respect, and gratitude.

FIGURE 2. (*continued*)

2. Reasons for doing right are needing to be good in one's own eyes and those of others, caring for others, and because if one puts oneself in the other person's place one would want good behavior from the self (Golden Rule).

Social Perspective. This stage takes the perspective of the individual in relationship to other individuals. A person at this stage is aware of shared feelings, agreements, and expectations, which take primacy over individual interests. The person relates points of view through the "concrete Golden Rule", putting oneself in the other person's shoes. He or she does not consider generalized "system" perspective.

STAGE 4.   The Stage of Social System and Conscience Maintenance

Content. The right is doing one's duty in society, upholding the social order, and maintaining the welfare of society or the group.

1. What is right is fulfilling the actual duties to which one has agreed. Laws are to be upheld except in extreme cases where they conflict with other fixed social duties and rights. Right is also contributing to society, the group, or institution.

2. The reasons for doing right are to keep the institution going as a whole, self-respect or conscience as meeting one's defined obligations, or the consequences: "What if everyone did it?"

Social Perspective. This stage differentiates societal point of view from interpersonal agreement or motives. A person at this stage takes the viewpoint of the system, which defines roles and rules. He or she considers individual relations in terms of place in the system.

LEVEL B/C/.   TRANSITIONAL LEVEL

This level is postconventional but not yet principled.

Content of Transition. At Stage 4½, choice is personal and subjective. It is based on emotions, conscience is seen as arbitrary and relative, as are ideas such as "duty" and "morally right."

Transitional Social Perspective. At this stage, the perspective is that of an individual standing outside of his own society and considering himself as an individual making decisions without a generalized commitment or contract with society. One can pick and choose obligations, which are defined by particular societies, but one has no principles for such choice.

LEVEL C.   POSTCONVENTIONAL AND PRINCIPLED LEVEL

Moral decisions are generated from rights, values, or principles that are (or could be) agreeable to all individuals composing or creating a society designed to have fair and beneficial practices.

(*continued*)

FIGURE 2. (*continued*)

STAGE 5. The Stage of Prior Rights and Social Contract or Utility

Content. The right is upholding the basic rights, values and legal contracts of a society, even when they conflict with the concrete rules and laws of the group.

1. What is right is being aware of the fact that people hold a variety of values and opinions, that most values and rules are relative to one's group. These "relative" rules should usually be upheld, however, in the interest of impartiality and because they are the social contract. Some nonrelative values and rights such as life, and liberty, however, must be upheld in any society and regardless of majority opinion.

2. Reasons for doing right are, in general, feeling obligated to obey the law because one has made a social contract to make and abide by laws for the good of all and to protect their own rights and the rights of others. Family, friendship, trust, and work obligations are also commitments or contracts freely entered into and entail respect for the rights of others. One is concerned that laws and duties be based on rational calculation of overall utility: "the greatest good for the greatest number."

Social Perspective. This stage takes a prior-to-society perspective — that of a rational individual aware of values and rights prior to social attachments and contracts. The person integrates perspectives by formal mechanisms of agreement, contract, objective impartiality, and due process. He or she considers the moral point of view and the legal point of view, recognizes they conflict, and finds it difficult to integrate them.

STAGE 6. The Stage of Universal Ethical Principles

Content. This stage assumes guidance by universal ethical principles that all humanity should follow.

1. Regarding what is right, Stage 6 is guided by universal ethical principles. Particular laws or social agreements are usually valid because they rest on such principles. When laws violate these principles, one acts in accordance with the principle. Principles are universal principles of justice, the equality of human rights and respect for the dignity of human beings as individuals. These are not merely values that are recognized, but are also principles used to generate particular decisions.

2. The reason for doing right is that, as a rational person, one has seen the validity of principles and has become committed to them.

Social Perspective. This stage takes the perspective of a moral point of view from which social arrangements derive or on which they are grounded. The perspective is that of any rational individual recognizing the nature of morality or the basic moral premise of respect for other persons as ends, not means.

Note: From THE PHILOSOPHY OF MORAL DEVELOPMENT by Lawrence Kohlberg. Copyright © 1981 by Lawrence Kohlberg. Reprinted by permission of Harper & Row, Publishers, Inc.

At the same time, there is another motif in Kohlberg which has raised doubts about his interactionism:

> Principles of justice are not only a social control to resolve conflicts in civil society, but are the reflection of an order inherent in both human nature and in the natural or cosmic order.[14]

> Stage 6 moral principles enjoining the uplifting of human personality are "eternal and natural law" in the sense that they are the universal outgrowth of the development of human nature.[15]

This second Kohlberg says that justice is a reality, independent of specific cultures and societies, and independent of the interaction of organism and environment; it is part of the natural order. Interaction may be necessary to reveal the fact of justice, but not to create it. According to this second Kohlberg, justice is not a matter of the relations between individuals, but of the relationship between parts of an individual's soul. Kohlberg's emphasis in this case is closer to a deontological morality concerned with *what ought to be*, rather than with a morality of agape concerned with love and care for one's fellowman. Indeed, Stage 6 morality is, in a certain sense, asocial and ahistorical ("Socrates, Martin Luther King, and Lincoln speak the same language and know no cultural boundaries"[16]), and according to Edmund Sullivan, it is less about interaction than it is about the duty of the individual soul.[17]

Thus, we find two conceptions of the relationship of the individual and the social in the moral sphere in Kohlberg: a deontological notion of morality as duty and obligation of the individual, and an interactionist notion of morality as the dynamic relationship of an individual in the context of specific social settings.

Kohlberg does not see these concepts as in conflict; his very task may be to attempt to synthesize these two apparently diverse theories.[18] Indeed, this attempt to synthesize two traditionally distinct philosophic theories is one of Kohlberg's most difficult and creative exercises.

MORAL PRINCIPLES

Kohlberg's system is one of the prominent contemporary exemplars of a moral theory that highlights the role of principles in the moral process. Kohlberg is regarded as a champion of a notion of morality that is rooted in a generalizable body of ultimate statements, rather than one based on convention, authority, or whim. The analysis of Kohlberg's writings reveals two distinct notions of 'moral principle'. His first sense of 'moral principle' is as a procedure or set of guidelines for confronting alternative moral choices and actions ("a generalized guide to choice,"[19] "a rule or method of choosing between legitimate activities,"[20] a universalistic and general basis for choice,"[21] "a universalizable impartial mode of deciding or judging"[22]). According to this usage, each of the six stages of moral development implies alternative forms or styles of choice in moral situations, for example, punishment, pleasure, acceptance, status, law, and justice. This notion of 'moral principle' does not refer to specific dictates or norms (such as "don't eat with your mouth open" or "don't use slugs in pay phones"), but rather, refers to procedural patterns for reflecting on moral problems.

The second usage of 'moral principle' in Kohlberg refers to the Stage 6 standard of justice as the desired criterion for resolving moral conflict. 'Moral principle' in this second sense refers to the universalizable, prescriptive value of justice. Whereas the former notion of 'moral principle' refers to choosing according to some sort of standards or criteria that are not arbitrary, the latter notion assumes that 'moral principle' means choosing according to the standard that is more "advanced," "mature," and valid — that is, justice. (At one point, Kohlberg indicates that the *content* of the principle of justice is what ultimately defines the "moral point of view."[23]) Thus, we find two senses of 'moral principle' in Kohlberg: as procedural *guides* for resolving moral conflicts *and* as the one, ultimate, definitive *content* of morality. In both cases, Kohlberg sees moral principles as the most general form of statements that do not dictate specific actions, but rather, that convey a mode of thinking that is then translatable into specific prescriptions and actions.

The second sense of moral principles as justice is formulated by Kohlberg in several ways:

Justice is a matter of equal and universal human rights.[24]

At advanced stages, the most basic principle of justice is equality. Treat every person's claim equally, regardless of the person.[25]

The primary substantive principle Stage 6 holds is the *respect for persons* principle: Treat each human being as an end in himself, as of ultimate worth. This also implies the following sub-principles: a) Liberty . . . b) Equality or justice . . . c) The greatest good or utility. . . . The ultimate Stage 6 principle of respect for persons, then, is the principle of justice.[26]

At heart, these [Stage 6 principles] are universal principles of *justice*, of the *reciprocity* and *equality* of human *rights*, and of respect for the dignity of human beings as *individual persons*.[27]

Analysts of Kohlberg have underscored the diversity of usages of the term 'justice' in his writings;[28] however, two characteristics are consistent in these various definitions: justice as involving the concern for the *welfare* of others and justice as involving the concern for the equal and fair treatment of others. Justice minimally means being concerned for the good of others and treating them equally.

Both notions of 'moral principle' in Kohlberg—as procedural guide for resolving moral conflict or as the content of justice—imply a rejection of either an emotivist or conventionalist conception of moral principles. Kohlberg rejects both the claim that moral principles are private statements of an individual's feelings or preferences and also the claim that they are expressions of the norms and standards of a group. In both cases for Kohlberg, a moral principle is a true, natural reality that is dependent neither on whim nor on collective consensus. Moral principles are not derivative or reducible phenomena that are dependent on other factors; they are self-existent and irreducible natural facts: "My analysis of moral judgement does not assume that moral judgements are really something else, but insists that they are prescriptive and *sui generis.*"[29]

Kohlberg, then, clearly rejects the notion of the relativity of moral principles, and he explains the apparent existence of variegated moral standards in terms of the fact that societies and individuals frequently confront the same moral problem from the differing perspectives of Stages 1 to 6. Thus, the aura of moral relativism is deceptive, for what really is happening are different developmental responses to a common problem. However, all such differences (and so-called relativism) disappear among Stage 6 personalities who share a unanimity and common perspective on value issues. Indeed, this unanimity and commonality—and not the apparent relativism and divergence of views—is the more accurate reflection of the state of moral principles.

Kohlberg's notion(s) of 'moral principle' have been criticized on several scores. As noted, some have claimed that his discussion of the concept of justice is overly general and ambiguous. Others claim that the approach comes to promulgate and inculcate a specific content in children, and however good justice may be, education should not impose or inculcate. Some critics suggest that Kohlberg is overly reductionist in attempting to distill all moral principles into 'justice', and as a result he neglects other worthy principles.[30] Several critics have indicated that Kohlberg's discussion of moral principles (and/or of moral education generally) is deficient because he neglects two extremely important related concepts, moral passion and moral habit.[31] Kohlberg, they say, tells us very little about the relationship between the morally principled person and the morally passionate and habituated person. Finally, the relativists argue that his picture of the world "as it really is" is topsy-turvy: difference of opinion and alternative values, rather than unanimity, are the true nature of moral reality today. Differences of opinion cannot be explained away by the phenomenon of more advanced or less advanced moral stages; the reality of modern life is the nonexistence of any one overriding and verifiably 'true' value, and the existence instead of competing value stances and alternatives. Some aspects of Kohlberg's treatment of 'moral principle' link him with colleagues who have appeared in this book; however, other aspects of his treatment of this concept make his system unique among contemporary theories of moral education.

REASON IN ETHICS

Kohlberg's theory is most popularly known as 'the cognitive-developmental approach to moral development and education' and his consistent emphasis on the role of cognition in morality squarely places him in the respected and prominent tradition of reflective morality.[32]

The cognitive aspect of morality for Kohlberg is not reserved for Stage 6; indeed, every one of the six stages of development implies the application of a distinctive pattern or system ('a logic') of thought to a moral problem. Thus, at Stage 1, children reflect on what to do in terms of what action will best prevent physical punishment; at Stage 3 they consider alternative options in terms of what they assume good boys or good girls are expected to do. At all levels of moral development, a process of moral reflection takes place and with a specific purpose: "the function of moral thinking is to resolve competing claims among individuals on the basis of a norm or principle."[33] Each stage, then, has a 'logic' or a 'reasoning pattern', and the child at all levels is a moral philosopher.

The process of moral thinking for Kohlberg has several characteristics. As we have seen, it is interactive, that is, moral thinking means the application of logical processes and operations by an individual to certain problems, experiences, and situations that are in the world. Moral thinking means to apply certain principles and practices to concrete structures and dilemmas. These procedures are intimately tied up with the concept of justice, and to think morally means to consider potential choices that would maximize the concern for others. This procedure should be impartial and unaffected by personal prejudices or group pressures. Kohlberg finds these procedures most conveniently summed up by terminology he derives from Kant and Hare: universalizability, prescriptivity, and impartiality.[34] To do moral thinking, then, is to apply impartially a procedure of logic that reflects the underlying principle of justice to real and specific human problems.

There have been three main criticisms of Kohlberg's conception of reason in ethics. The first argues with the very notion of moral reasoning that he has adopted. According to this argument, there are several theories of moral reasoning and Kohlberg has opted for one tradition, and although it is certainly a respected one, it is not necessarily the only one.[35] Thus, Aristotelians or Deweyians would suggest their notions of reasoning as better alternatives.

A second line of criticism argues that Kohlberg's notion of moral reasoning is far less procedural than he suggests and what it really constitutes is the imposition of a particular ethic or value. Thus, instead of encouraging open reflection on moral alternatives, Kohlberg actually constructs — very much as Socrates did to Meno — a dialectic pattern that manipulates the child into accepting a certain value.

The third criticism focuses on the aforementioned neglect of the role of affect in moral reasoning.[36] According to this charge, a theory of moral reasoning must explain its relationship to moral feeling and senses in order to be truly comprehensive, and this is not done by Kohlberg.

Kohlberg has responded to all three criticisms. He reacts to the first point by indicating that it is true that there are different forms of reasoning, which in fact parallel the stages of moral development. However, it has been empirically shown that one stage or logic of moral reasoning is more inclusive, adequate, and sophisticated than the others; it does what all previous logics do and more. Thus, Kohlberg argues that he has not arbitrarily chosen one logic rather than another because he happens to like it, but because this particular logic has proven itself to be the most developed and universal.

Kohlberg's response to the imposition argument is that the development of natural traits and abilities is not imposition or indoctrination, it is growth. Moral reasoning is not a particular whim or preference of Lawrence Kohlberg; it is a natural, universal dimension of human existence and, hence, its stimulation is the goal of education. Socrates did not impose values on Meno; he helped him grow by developing Meno's own natural abilities.

Kohlberg claims that he has not neglected will and feeling in moral development; rather, they are part of the process of moral reasoning. Thus, he would argue that the exemplars of Stage 6 morality — Gandhi, Martin Luther King, and Jesus — are proof that 'the cognitively developed' person is also a person of great moral passion and feeling. Will and emotion are certainly not irrelevant factors in moral development; but rather than existing as independent factors of morality, they are part of and flow from general cognitive-moral development. The Stage 6 person who has reached the heights of cognitive moral development is also a person of great moral passion.

FORM AND CONTENT

Kohlberg's system makes the case that moral development should be seen in terms of the development of certain characteristic *forms* or *structures* of thinking, rather than in terms of the transmission or inculcation of specific contents or behaviors:

> I am arguing that a criterion of adequacy must take account of the fact that morality is a unique *sui generis* realm. If it is unique, its uniqueness must be defined by general formal criteria, so my multi-ethical conception is formalistic. I define morality in terms of the formal character of a moral judgement, method, or point of view, rather than in terms of its content.[37]

> In this sense, one can define a moral judgement as "moral" without considering its content (the action judged) and without considering whether it agrees with our own judgements or standards.[38]

Early Kohlberg repeatedly criticizes the "good boy—good girl" or "bag of virtues" approach to moral education in which the task of moral education is seen as the transmission and inculcation of specific virtues or behaviors. Morality is not mainly a collection of specific norms or deeds; it is, rather, a perspective, style, a point of view. This style or point of view is best described by the notion of Stage 6 morality—which, as we saw in the previous two sections, implies a certain style of principled moral reasoning.

Does Kohlberg's system focus on morality mainly as a structure and style of judgment as it claims, rather than on specific contents? Kohlberg's system is clearly not about the inculcation of specific behaviors or norms; he consistently rejects the notion of moral education as teaching a specific bag of virtues. Even in the late Kohlberg, where we find less attack on morality as specific contents and greater encouragement of the development of specific moral actions, the emphasis remains on the actions as exemplars of a style or procedure.[39] Contents do not come to replace morality as a style or form; instead, they are the vehicle, conduit, and the laboratory for exemplifying that style. Thus, there clearly is a sense in which morality refers to a procedure or an approach that has certain formal characteristics, for example, universalizability, prescriptivity, and impartiality, and that serves as a method of confronting certain sorts of problems. Why, then, do critics continually argue that Kohlberg's higher levels of moral reasoning are as much a content as a procedure? For example:

> Even if the superior conformity of later stages to certain formal features of moral judgments shows them to be "so far forth" superior, that does not get us very far. What Kohlberg really wants most to recommend to our accept-

ance is the principle of justice (in his interpretation) as a supreme moral principle.[40]

There are, indeed, formal characteristics for moral reasoning at Kohlberg's advanced stages; however, there also is the additional component of justice. Kohlberg regards this component as a formal quality, whereas the critics regard it as a substantive moral principle. Their argument is not with the principle itself, but with its delineation as a formal characteristic. (Indeed, this discussion is reminiscent of the critiques of Wilson's moral components, especially PHIL, which the critics argued is a substantive moral principle rather than a formal characteristic.)

It is certainly clear that Kohlberg sees moral reasoning as having formal characteristics; it is not clear that it has *only* formal characteristics. In fact, what Kohlberg really seems to be proposing is an argument basic to Dewey's theory of morality, namely that the form-content dichotomy is meaningless. Indeed, Kohlberg clearly asserts this at one point when he indicates that "Now it is clear that our conception of moral principle implies that one cannot ultimately separate form and content in moral analysis."[41] To engage in the *form* of advanced moral reasoning means to apply the general *content* of justice;[42] the form of moral reasoning indicates the content of morality, and the content of morality necessitates the application of a certain form of reasoning.

Kohlberg suggests that he is part of a tradition described as the formalist school in ethics (e.g., Hare, Peters, and Rawls); however, a closer look at that school and at Kohlberg reveals that it is not simply about form in the sense of driving a car or weaving a rug. Kohlberg (and probably the formalists) certainly rejects a notion of morality as specific dictates and behaviors and affirms a notion of morality as an approach; however, the approach at its most advanced stages includes and is very much determined by the content of justice.

ACTION

Kohlberg reflects an honored and debated tradition in moral philosophy that argues that virtue cannot be divided into intellectual and behavioral (or moral) components as Aristotle would have us believe, but rather, that action is, as Plato argues, an inherent and irreducible aspect of moral thinking. Thus, the Platonic-Kohlbergian approach does not assume that its emphasis on moral deliberation is at the expense of moral action; instead, it is an emphasis on both moral deliberation and action: "Persons at a higher level of moral development not only reason better, but they act in accordance with their judgements."[43]

The argument of this school is that genuine moral thinking is or directly leads to doing; that is, that moral knowledge and thinking by its very nature results in moral action (a Stage 6 person acts in certain ways), and part of the process of moral deliberation is the consideration and rehearsal of certain actions as opposed to certain others. Thus, Kohlberg claims that his system clearly does deal with moral action, but not as training in the performance of sets of specific behaviors. The appropriate route to moral action is not through drill or rote repetition, but rather, through reflection and deliberation.

Kohlberg's position on action has been criticized both philosophically and educationally. The philosophers have cited alternative Aristotelian traditions that posit the existence of two spheres — intellectual and behavioral — and they argue that Kohlberg has neglected the latter. R. S. Peters claims that habit is a legitimate concept in moral education that does not replace nor contradict reason in the moral sphere, but instead is a necessary and valuable step in the process of the development of the reflective moral person.[44]

Some psychological critics have argued that moral action is the result of action tendencies and of their interplay, which are not mediated by such cognitive processes as moral definitions, moral beliefs, and moral reasoning. Augusto Blasi, for example, asserts that "there are in each person a number of habits, behavioral traits, or generalized action tendencies leading to a variety of specific behaviors (e.g., sharing, helping, cooperating, sympathizing) that in many cultures are placed in the same generic class of moral action."[45] Educational critics have claimed that deliberation and reflection do not seem to have resulted in better behaviors; more intelligent or reflective people and societies do not necessarily seem to be any better in their morality.

Kohlberg has listened attentively to discussions and criticisms on this topic, and he has both defended his Platonic assumptions while also introducing revisions into his system.[46] His first response to the critics has been to restate and defend the Platonic position. Kohlberg's argument is that better thinking implies better acting; Jesus, Martin Luther King, and Socrates did not only think well, they acted in uniquely good ways. Higher moral stages are advanced stages of thinking *and* of doing.[47]

Kohlberg later admits the need for a concern for "value content as well as structure, behavior as well as reasoning" in moral education. Schools must teach value content as well as dialectic. This is not instead of or ultimately more important than the moral judgment function, but it is a legitimate function that Kohlberg claims he initially underemphasized.

Thus, we find in Kohlberg's more recent writings a pedagogic shift toward greater emphasis on the development of specific behaviors and actions as a dimension of moral education. This has manifested itself in two changed directions in his pedagogic writings: (1) more emphasis on school setting and activities that enable students to actually learn to do and apply moral thinking;[48] (2) more emphasis on real rather than hypothetical moral dilemmas.[49] In both cases, Kohlberg suggests that schools should engage in educational activities to develop moral reasoning procedures as well as activities to develop moral experiences and behaviors. This pedagogic adjustment is accompanied by an adjustment in his system of six moral stages to five, in which emphasis is focused on a social morality of shared obligations.[50]

The charge that more deliberation has not led to better people is, of course, one of those perennial charges made against innovations in education. Thus, Dewey's "progressive education" was held responsible for the drug culture, the failure of America to get into outer space before the Russians, and long hair. Clearly, the criticism does not reflect any systematic nor scientific type of educational evaluation; indeed, cognitive-developmental moral education has probably not sustained enough trial to warrant any generalizations about its success or failure. Hence, Kohlberg cannot yet be held responsible for the goods or evils of the 1970s and 1980s!

THE MORALLY EDUCATED PERSON

Who is the morally educated person according to the cognitive-developmental approach? He/she is a person who draws upon a combination of characteristics to confront a moral situation: reflection, principles, the value of justice, a disposition to act, and the awareness of and interaction with a social setting. The morally educated person has learned how to reflect on a (moral) problem that arises in a social setting, consider the various alternatives, reach a resolution in terms of the most general principle of justice (rather than on the basis of custom, law, or whim), and translate this deliberation into a deed. The morally educated person for Kohlberg has both learned the process of moral deliberation and judgment, and operationalizes the process *so as to realize the principle of justice in the world*. The morally educated person is like Jesus, Socrates, Janus Korczak, and Martin Luther King in emulating their *processes* of moral resolution *as well as* their moral lives.

Most of these components of the morally educated person have surfaced in other theories we have examined so far; however, one element that distinguishes Kohlberg's notion of the morally educated person is its content. Indeed, of all the theories we have examined, it is only Kohlberg who gives us a clearly articulated value content for moral education (as well as a specific list of exemplars of moral being). While Durkheim is often regarded as the traditionalist of twentieth-century moral education, in fact, he does not present either a specific moral creed or a pantheon of moral heroes. It is a contemporary American social scientist of moral education who presents the most paradigmatically normative theory and practice of moral education in the twentieth century.

INDOCTRINATION

Kohlberg suggests that there are three possible types of activities related to the teaching of morality.[51]

1. education for moral relativity
2. indoctrination
3. cognitive-developmental moral education

He argues that the first two are inadequate as approaches to moral education and proposes the third as the viable theory of moral education.

Education for moral relativity is an approach that accepts the fact of many different moral standards and perspectives as a given and turns it into a value; consequently, it regards the function of schooling as the presentation of these various perspectives. It is an approach that is very much in touch with the fact of moral pluralism and committed to an open presentation of various perspectives. This approach is reluctant to impose any one perspective on children, since it is not convinced of the authority or conclusiveness of any one view.

Kohlberg agrees with this approach's sensitivity to pluralistic moral perspectives and to its reluctance to impose ideologies on the young. However, the error of this approach is its assumption that the fact of many moral perspectives necessarily implies that they are all equally legitimate. The fact that there are many moral stances does not mean that they are all equally compelling, just as the fact of the existence of many brands of audio equipment does not mean that they are all of equal worth. In fact, these alternate moral stances are not parallel perspectives, but rather, reflect different developmental stages on a moral hierarchy. The various moral perspectives are, in fact, different levels of moral development in which some are less advanced and others are more advanced. Consequently, it is miseducative to teach each of the perspectives as equal and parallel options; the educator's task should be to advance the child to that level or perspective that is the most advanced. Moral relativity as an educational approach does not do this; instead, it leaves the child in a moral abyss and does not help him to advance to the most sophisticated moral perspective.

'Indoctrination' goes to the opposite extreme. It assumes the existence of one moral truth for which it does not offer any conclusive or verifiable truth. 'Indoctrination' reflects the attempt to impose from without a body of truths for which no evidence exists. Thus, 'indoctrination' is a faulty educational activity for two reasons. First, it is rooted in nonverifiable, nonconclusive 'truths' or theories, and education should not transmit theories that are not conclusively verifiable. Second, 'indoctrination' is insensitive to the fact that education implies growth and development from within rather than imposition from without. 'Indoctrination' neglects the indispensable role of the child as his/her own teacher.

Thus, what bothers Kohlberg about 'indoctrination' is not its directive nature, but rather, the nature of its *contents* and its *methods* of direction. In fact, Kohlberg's theory of education is clearly committed to a belief in the validity of direction, on the condition that it is done in a way that respects the child's integrity and reflects verifiable contents. Hence, a moral education that comes to direct or stimulate a child's moral development in the direction of justice is eminently legitimate; it is neither an imposition nor is it neutral. The cognitive-developmental approach is legitimate because its contents are part of the natural order and because its methods respect the ability of the child to reflect and choose. Hence, Kohlberg's notion of 'indoctrination' is close to the 'content' school (as reflected, for example, in early Wilson),[52] which sees this activity as very much related to the transmission of dogmas or nonverifiable contents. Kohlberg is much less afraid of a directive education than advocates of VC or some of the antimoral educationists are.[53] Direction is legitimate if it reflects movement toward the natural order. Education for moral relativity is an abdication of any concern for direction, and 'indoctrination' reflects an attempt to replace natural direction with a superimposition of personal or private beliefs. Cognitive-developmental moral education remedies the deficiencies of both of these approaches.

Kohlberg has recently modified his staunch antiindoctrination stand, arguing that moral reasoning stage development is a goal—but not the only goal of moral education. He now allows that schools must also teach specific value contents, and in becoming agents of socialization and advocacy they approach indoctrination of necessity: "I no longer hold these negative views of indoctrinative moral education and I now believe that the concepts guiding moral education must be partly 'indoctrinative'."[54]

However, this surely does not mean that Kohlberg has changed his notion of 'indoctrination' or that he now legitimizes it as moral education. Rather, he has softened his original, nonindoctrinary position to make room for the legitimacy of the transmission of some specific contents and behaviors. Indeed, the shift is essentially pedagogic and pragmatic and is not a radical reformation of the Kohlbergian hierarchy.

THE TEACHER

One of the reasons for the great popularity of Kohlberg is his precisely delineated and humane conception of the teacher as moral educator. Kohlberg carefully outlines the parameters of the teacher's role in moral education, establishing reasonable expectations and limitations.

The essential task of the teacher is to contribute to the process of moral development, that is, to serve as a facilitator for the cognitive-developmental moral growth of the child. Thus, the essence of the teacher's task is to advance a process of thinking, judgment, and deliberation. This is to be put into effect by a series of carefully developed procedures, which while flexible are at the same time precisely structured. The teacher's function is neither haphazard nor laissez-faire; rather, it is a carefully elaborated Socratic style of probing, teaching, suggesting, underscoring, and directing.

This general function of the teacher encompasses four subtasks.[55] First, the teacher should help students to focus on and confront genuine moral conflicts; this can be done either by utilization of normal classroom materials or by systematic presentation of hypothetical moral dilemmas. The second task is to help students reflect on the alternative ways of reasoning about moral conflicts and resolving them. This function involves helping students to see moral judgment as related to reflective processes. The third task is to help students to critically reflect on the adequacies and inadequacies of the thinking processes that they have employed. In this case, the teacher comes to encourage a metaethical, second-order activity of self-reflection on the individual's own thinking processes. The final task is to suggest to students a procedure of reflection and resolution that is more efficient than their current method. The function here is to enable students to "bump into" a stage of moral judgment at least one level higher than their current stage. Kohlberg's underlying pedagogic assumption is that when someone comes into contact with a more efficient and effective stage he/she will adapt it and thereby advance morally. It is crucial that the teacher use both suggestions and intervention at this stage and at the same time not be imposing. Kohlberg repeatedly suggests that the essential style or mood of the teacher should be Socratic, which he understands as patient, listening, and receptive as well as critical, questioning, and even aggressive. Both sides of the Socratic method are important if the child is to advance on the ladder of moral development.

Kohlberg's recent emphasis on a moral socialization function of moral education also has implications for the teacher's role — "the educator must be a socializer, teaching value content and behavior, not merely a Socratic facilitator of judgement."[56] Thus, the teacher, particularly in the context of the 'just community' school, may now be expected to be both Socrates and Jesus, Plato and Martin Luther King!

There are two contexts in which the teacher should function as moral educator. In his earlier writings, Kohlberg stresses the role of the teacher in the context of discussions of hypothetical moral dilemmas and in the teaching of formal curriculum units. In this case, the teacher utilizes a series of carefully constructed and tested hypothetical moral situations or real historical and sociological situations as the basis for the four didactic activities just discussed.[57] In more recent writings, Kohlberg has focused on the role of the teacher as citizen and member of the 'just community'.[58] In this community, the teacher utilizes the real issues in the daily life of the school and the child as a basis for moral discussion and reflection.

Kohlberg's teacher is not explicitly burdened with the responsibility of being an exemplar of a particular morality, or a spokesperson of a particular society's values. Thus, we do not find in Kohlberg specific prescriptions for how teachers should dress, talk, or behave outside of school. Indeed, he is critical of such attempts as the *madrich* or counselor in the Israeli kibbutz, where moral roles and behaviors for the educator are too precisely delineated.[59]

The general direction of Kohlberg's moral teacher is as moral philosopher rather than saint or priest. In that sense, Kohlberg's teacher might seem to be closer to Wilson than to Durkheim. But at the same time, Kohlberg's teacher-heroes are ultimately more than (only occasionally far less than) moral philosophers. Jesus is a reflective figure, but more overwhelmingly an exemplar of personal life-style; Martin Luther King is as much characterized by his charisma, rhetoric, mystique, and deeds, as by his deliberative style. This other side of the teacher is most dramatically underscored in the epilogue to *Philosophy of Moral Development*, which focuses on Janus Korczak as moral teacher. Kohlberg's point in this brief essay is that Korczak was a great moral educator because of his process *and* his personality.

> [Korczak's] life illustrates the fact that the truest and most inspired moral educators possess something more than a philosophy of justice — they possess a "Stage 7" ethical and religious perspective of agape. . . . This Stage 7 moral educator wisely did not attempt to explicitly preach or morally educate for "Stage 7" . . . this vision is communicated by example, not by systematic education.[60]

Korczak's role was that of facilitator, priest, rabbi, father, believer; he helped people to reflect *and* he inspired them.

One of the reasons for Kohlberg's great appeal to teachers is, as noted, the clear, precisely delineated, and limited role he prescribes for them as moral deliberators and philosophers. However, a careful reading of Kohlberg reveals that his conception of the teacher is more involved and demanding than we might have thought, for Kohlberg also wants the teacher to have the heart of Jesus, the charisma of Martin Luther King, and the exemplary behavior of Janus Korczak.

PEDAGOGY

Kohlberg's moral pedagogy does not pretend to be original; rather, it draws upon and reflects some very old and some very new pedagogical theories. Moreover, it is not static, and Kohlberg has over the years adjusted, modified, and added to his practical approaches. Kohlberg indicates that his initial direction in a practice of moral education drew upon the research of his student, Moshe Blatt, who was interested in examining the extent to which carefully controlled classroom discussions of moral issues could lead to moral stage development. The so-called Blatt effect refers to the conclusion that one-fourth to one-half of students who participated in verbal moral discussions under controlled conditions for a year advanced at least one moral stage.[61] The three characteristics of the controlled situations were as follows:

1. The presentation of controversial moral dilemmas in areas that arouse cognitive disagreement among students.
2. A mixture of students in the class who are at different moral stages.
3. An open, challenging Socratic teaching style.

The first thrust, then, of Kohlberg's moral pedagogy concentrated on critical discussion of moral issues, utilizing a carefully developed set of hypothetical moral dilemmas. Many teaching aids for presenting these dilemmas were developed over the years, for example, filmstrips, instructional units, and ditto masters.[62] Indeed, in the early Kohlberg, we find an overt resistance to regular, formal teaching of morality; rather, Kohlberg saw moral pedagogy as periodic and as a style to be incorporated into the regular life of the school.

Kohlberg's pedagogic interests have moved in recent years into three areas: (1) curriculum, (2) participatory school settings, and (3) teacher training. In the 1970s, Kohlberg's work begins to reflect a much more systematic concern with curriculum, both in the specific sphere of morality as well as in other areas. Thus, curricula of moral education begin to emerge, influenced by developments in the "new curriculum,"[63] and especially in the area of social studies. For example, the Carnegie-Mellon Education project integrates the Kohlbergian approach with the teaching of social studies and English. This development reflected a sense that educational theory must find expression in practice, and curriculum is one of the prominent areas of practice. This shift is evidence of a more sustained approach to moral reasoning in the curriculum and of the movement away from hypothetical dilemmas to real situations. While hypothetical dilemmas (e.g., Heinz's dilemma), make for good discussion, they were often regarded as too abstract and distant from actual situations.

In addition, Kohlberg became much more sensitive to the notion of the nonformal or hidden curriculum as a factor in moral education. He began to turn his attention to the potential impact of the life of the school as an arena for working out moral issues "the character or 'moral atmosphere' of a group or community."[64] Kohlberg's interest in this area does not imply a return to a classical notion of the school as a hothouse for inculcating "good deeds"; rather, he focuses on the school's potential to serve as a laboratory for moral deliberation and action vis à vis issues related to the students' own lives. Thus, the functioning of the school as a participatory democracy is a means of enabling young people to reflect upon and carry out morality.

Another shift that occurs in Kohlberg's practical programs for moral education is his retrenchment to a Stage 5 and Stage 4 moral education. On the occasion of the 1976 bicentennial of the United States, Kohlberg lamented the apparent paucity and perhaps nonexistence of Stage 6 people ("My longitudinal subjects, still adolescents in 1968, had come to adulthood by 1976, but none had reached the sixth stage.")[65] This development was paralleled by the decline in basic civic interest among young people, that is, their decreased respect for the value of society and its basic values, and the increased concern for privatism and negation of the community as a value. Hence, Kohlberg in the late 1970s and early 1980s increasingly called for a Stage 4 civic education that would educate young people for participation in the community and the development of behaviors of good citizenship and social concern. Kohlberg regards the 'just community', the participatory school democracy, and the cluster school as particularly valuable devices for this purpose.

Finally, Kohlberg in the 1970s began to express a concern for the role of teacher training and in-service training in the sphere of moral education. Two aspects of teacher training are stressed: (1) a concern (à la Wilson) for the philosophic understanding by the teacher of the theoretical bases of the moral sphere and of cognitive-developmental moral theory and (2) exercises and case studies in translating this theory into the practical language and experiences of teachers. Kohlberg is critical of his initial emphasis on the theory of cognitive development of moral education at the expense of the practical, and he subsequently calls for a return to the situation of the teacher as the starting point for teacher education.[66] Thus, we are witness to a proliferation of books, workshops, lectures, pamphlets, and scoring manuals (paralleling the VC explosion) concerned with making Kohlberg accessible to the teacher.

CONCLUSION

Kohlberg has clearly emerged as a dominant, mid-late, twentieth-century figure in the theory and practice of moral education, and he has increasingly become the starting point from which most new theories emerge and/or react. The extent of his influence is certainly related to the fact that his work is not limited to specific disciplinary boundaries; it is equally debated in university departments of philosophy, psychology, sociology, education, and in teacher's rooms or at conventions and staff meetings, and on the pages of popular journals and newspapers. In that sense, Durkheim, Kohlberg, and Dewey (who joins us in Chapter 7) are *the* twentieth-century exemplars of the attempt to present a total, comprehensive, and integrative theory and practice of morality and moral education.

Chapter 6

AGAINST
MORAL EDUCATION

WE HAVE SEEN in the previous chapters that there is disagreement in twentieth-century education as to what moral education should be; however, each of the positions we have examined shares in common the belief that moral education is a legitimate activity of schools. Thus, while Durkheim, Wilson, VC, and Kohlberg disagree as to what it means to carry out moral education, they all concur that the attempt to engage in this enterprise (whatever it may be) in schools is a proper educational activity.

There is, however, an educational tradition that argues otherwise, contending that moral education is *not* a legitimate activity of schools and that it should, in fact, have no place therein.[1] This tradition spans centuries of educational and political writings, and thousands of miles of geography and culture. It is represented by such names as Godwin, Rousseau, Tolstoy, Sterner, Paul Robin, Ferrer, Kropotkin, Robert Owen, Ivan Illich, Everet Reimer, Paulo Freire. It cuts across national boundaries, ideological positions, and historical periods, and constitutes a remarkably long and dynamic educational tradition. This tradition has surfaced in American education most vividly in recent times in the radical educational reform literature of the 1960s[2] and in the revisionist educational histories of the 1970s.[3]

In fact, the "anti-moral education tradition" is not one unified movement at all; it is an amalgam of diverse views on society, man, economy, and education. Indeed, it often reflects a strange compendium of strikingly different views, and we find in this tradition rejection of moral education by anarchists,[4] socialists,[5] atheists,[6] and Christians.[7] The educational historian, Michael Katz, and the educational reformers of the 1960s agree that moral education in schools is a form of imposition and indoctrination, yet the former criticizes the latter for being overly conciliatory and conservative.[8] Illich wants to de-school society in order to create a new, more egalitarian social order, whereas Leonard is interested in changing schools so as to maximize the ecstatic experience of the individual.[9]

This ambiguity is not reserved for the theory of the anti-moral education movement—it also surfaces in the actual practice of radical and alternative schools. Thus, Avrich tells us that the founders of the modern school movement in the United States were an assortment of anarchists, atheists, socialists, syndicalists, and single taxers.[10] The New York Modern School was founded in the name and on behalf of the principles of the great Spanish anarchist martyr Francisco Ferrer, and one of its first and most prominent teachers was a young socialist named Will Durant!

Hence, all of those who opposed moral education throughout the world and the centuries do not necessarily share similar views on larger questions of man, society, ethics, and education, just as those who support moral education also are not united on these issues. The one issue on which there is agreement among the host of views we are loosely calling the anti-moral education tradition is the idea that schools should not engage in this activity. These various disparate views share the belief that, for various reasons, it would be better if schools did not attempt to regard moral education as one of their prominent tasks and responsibilities. This tradition, of course, stands in sharp contrast to the approaches represented in the past four chapters of this book, where arguments for moral education as one of the main tasks and responsibilities of schools are given.

The phrase "the anti-moral educationists" is itself misleading, since the diverse population to which I am referring does not always agree about what it is against! Many of these writers share the belief that any attempt of any kind by any type of school to engage in moral education is inappropriate. Some writers, for example, Neil, Tolstoy, and Illich, are really arguing for alternative models of schools rather than the total abrogation of the enterprise. The socialists ultimately are opposed to the specific moral code that most "bourgeois" schools teach, but not to the activity per se. Others argue about the legitimacy of moral education in public or community controlled schooling; that is, they argue that it is improper to impose a specific morality in schools sponsored by public groups and funds. (This group affirms the right of private groups to establish and fund their own schools as they see fit.) Thus, our task will include clarifying what exactly is being opposed or rejected within the sphere of moral education.

The analytic task we are proposing to undertake is particularly difficult because of the broad constellation of theories that comprise the 'tradition' and because of the paucity of analytic material on this topic.[11] Indeed, the often great disparities between constituent schools of this tradition led us to consider the possibility of focusing on one theory alone (e.g., Tolstoy or Illich or Neil) as was our pattern up to now. The limitation of such a pattern of analysis is that it would focus on only one type of argument against moral education, whereas in fact what is precisely of interest in this tradition is the broad range of quite distinct arguments. Hence, in this chapter we will view an introductory map — rendered in broad and tentative strokes — of categorical parameters for several diverse theories. Although it may seem presumptuous to cover the material in this manner, to have omitted this tradition would have been to neglect a major, contemporary statement about moral education.

This approach obviously necessitates the suspension in this chapter of the conceptual prism that we have employed so far in our analysis of theories. This prism is inappropriate in dealing with the anti-moral educationists for technical reasons — it would be far beyond the proportions of this volume to analyze eight or ten theories according to our nine parameters, and for substantive reasons — some of our participating theories are short, idiosyncratic statements that do not have the conceptual depth or quantity of the writings of Durkheim or Kohlberg. Hence, instead of looking at the 'tradition' in terms of nine categories of moral philosophy and education, we shall briefly describe five categories of arguments against moral education: the epistemological; the individualist; the socialist; the empirical evaluative; and the structural.

There is a prejudice that occasionally appears with respect to "anti-moral educationists" that I think should be laid to rest prior to such an analysis. The very act of "opposing" moral education is sometimes regarded as similar to a rejection of God, motherhood, and apple pie, and those who do it are regarded as alternatively 'libertine', 'reckless', 'irresponsible', 'immoral', 'vulgar', and 'perverted'. I would like to urge that such preconceptions be put aside; the fact is that the argument of the anti-moral educationists is not against 'morality' per se, but against its appearance in public education. The fact of being against moral education does not turn such people into immoralists. (Indeed, many of the anti-moral educationists appear to be very gentle, humane, and decent people who love children and with whom I imagine you would feel most comfortable leaving your child! Meet Francisco Ferrer, Ivan Illich, Carl Bereiter, and S. Yizhar in their books; I suspect you will find them to be nice people. Moreover, we have all met so called 'moral people' who want to "do" or "engage in" moral education, and who have very frequently been terribly frightening!) Indeed, it may well be the case that the opposition of the anti-moral educationists is best understood as an educational stance adopted *in the name of morality* rather than against it. In any case, we can come to know this school better if the prejudice described is avoided.

FIVE ARGUMENTS AGAINST MORAL EDUCATION

The Epistemological

One prominent argument against moral education in schools is rooted in the belief that this activity is illegitimate since schools should only teach verifiable and objective bodies of knowledge, and moral issues, morality, and moral knowledge are not verifiable or objective in the same sense as the sciences. This argument reflects the epistemological position that there are different spheres of human experience and knowing, and some are more publicly and objectively verifiable than others. The more positivist strain of this tradition would argue that there ultimately is one true, best way of knowing; some of the less positivist stances content themselves with talking about different spheres of knowledge or realms of meaning. Among the spheres most often regarded as either nonverifiable or not agreed upon are morality, politics, and religion. Hence, the claim is that one would not want to impose either subjective or not agreed upon opinions in these three sensitive areas on children. Rather, education should deal with only publicly verifiable and agreed upon contents, often characterized as 'scientific' or 'rational'.

This position is argued by Wilson in his discussion of the nature of indoctrination when he claims that schools should only teach facts and arguments for which there is publicly accepted evidence, that is, "evidence which any rational person would regard as sufficient"; therefore, this position excludes the study of religion or morals since they are not epistemologically of the same quality.[12] Ferrer argues that rational education ("the scientific development of reason") is the key to genuine individual and social liberation from dogma and authority.[13] Bruce Calvert, Director of the Rational School in Chicago, described rational education as the concern "to train the mind to grasp the facts of nature and organize them into an individual working conception of the cosmos. It was to free the student from obsession and superstition, to throw upon him the integrity of his own thought."[14]

A clear expression of this position is found in Carl Bereiter's *Must We Educate?*[15] Bereiter's position is that education (and moral education) is improper because it involves the imposition of ideals, values, and opinions of teachers and principals on children. He distinguishes between three types of school-based activities:

1. Child care—the task of guaranteeing the safety and comfort of a child when he is out of his parent's care;
2. Training—the transmission and development of specific skills which are necessary for one's subsequent functioning (e.g., the 3 R's);
3. Education—the attempt to impose values, attitudes, and behaviours of a society on the child so as to make him into a socialized agent of that society (i.e., "to mold citizens and shape the next generation").[16]

Bereiter regards activities 1 and 2 as legitimate functions of schools; he considers activity 3 to be morally wrong. In terms of the epistemological argument against moral education, activity 2 is relevant; it is based on the assumption that there are certain bodies of knowledge (what Bereiter has called skills) that are public, agreed upon, and functional. Such skills include reading, writing, and arithmetic, as well as such things as the learning of nonmanipulative social skills, learning how to speak honestly what is on your mind, learning how to take the point of view of others, and learning how to distinguish between a viola and a violin.[17] Bereiter contends that such skill knowledge is a legitimate content of education because "to acquire such skills is not to become a certain kind of person, but rather to acquire a greater capacity of becoming the sort of person one desires to be. . . . There are manifold ways of increasing personal power and personal options which don't require that we decide in advance what kind of people children should become."[18] Such training is not immoral because it does not come to shape the whole person according to some speculative world-view, but rather to provide him with true, non-speculative knowledge (i.e., skills) which will enable him ultimately to be his/her own molder and shaper.

Thus, the epistemological argument assumes that moral education is wrong because of the speculative, non-scientific, non-agreed upon nature of the contents it comes to impose on the young. According to this argument, education should only deal with contents or procedures which are true, objective, scientific, rational: that is, which are not the private, speculative viewpoints of individuals or groups.

The Individualist

A second argument against moral education in schools contends that the individual is the primary unit in life, and schooling should be concerned with the liberation and autonomy of the individual. It opposes moral education in schools, since it regards this activity as a tool of the state or the group to impose its own values and to perpetuate itself. One aspect of this approach is its commitment to the notion of ownership of self,[19] that is, the belief that children have within themselves the resources to become free, choosing agents, if they are not impeded or imposed upon from without. The popular metaphor of this approach is the child as a flower to be periodically watered and given sun, but mostly to be protected from outside forces which would tamper with or distort it.[20]

There are several subcategories within this general concern for the individual and fear of his manipulation by outside forces. Some, for example, Leonard and perhaps Tolstoy, focus on the mystical, nonrational, ecstatic nature of the individual, and consequently the expression of self or the heightening of consciousness becomes the main educational concern.

The assumption is that there is a unique human sphere that lies within and that ultimately, under the right "conditions," can be brought to the surface. This educational approach reflects the assumption of an ethical truth inherent in the person, which education should help to bring to the fore.

A second subcategory of the individualist strain focuses on the centrality of personal expression and preference per se as an educational ideal. This approach sees education as a means of heightening personal expression, desire, and feeling as values in themselves. Ethically, it reflects the emotivist assumption of the personal and idiosyncratic nature of moral preferences, as opposed to some objective set of criteria.

A third subcategory emphasizes the ability of people to reason and argues that we should provide children with the tool that will become the ultimate source of their redemption, that is, reason. This approach emphasizes people's unique ability to solve problems and to live via their rational skills, and education should focus on the development and honing of these skills. This category most closely reflects the prescriptivist ethical stance that emphasizes morality as a process with certain formal dimensions.

What unites the subcategories of the individualist school is their rejection of the legitimacy of the public school's role in moral education as a vehicle of imposition upon and manipulation of the individual:

> The rejection of the public school represents one of the important themes in the historical development of radical forms of education from William Godwin in the eighteenth century to Ivan Illich in the twentieth, and has been premised on the idea that schools come into being as a means of shaping the moral and social beliefs of the population for the benefit of a dominant elite.[21]

According to the approach, moral education impedes genuine moral development in the young, rather than advancing it. Neil expresses this point in a radical fashion when he argues that instruction in morals only subjugates the child to outside authority and convention, rather than enabling him/her to develop the genuine sources of morality which are within each of us. According to Neil, it is only when moral instruction is *prevented* or stopped that moral education can begin:

> I believe that it is moral instruction that makes a child bad. I find that when I smash the moral instruction a bad boy has received, he automatically becomes a good boy.[22]

Just as there are different notions of the development and the liberation of the individual, so there are different notions of the nature of this imposition and manipulation. Ferrer and Bakunin objected to the manipulation of the child by the church;[23] Illich opposes the manipulation of the child by the consumer market and the export mentality;[24] Bowles and Gintis object to manipulation by the forces of capitalist economy;[25] Firestone points to the manipulation of education by male stereotypes.[26] All share the belief that moral education in public schools is doomed to be a tool of some specific interest group (whether Christian, male, white, capitalist, or technocrat) that will subjugate students and attempt to impose values on them.

This particular approach would propose two solutions to the problem of moral education. One solution is to do away with schools completely (i.e., the de-schooling of society), since schools are regarded as forever doomed to be oppressive. Thus, this individualist view is critical of liberal and reform tendencies, which it sees as partial modifications and surface improvements to a basically evil system. (Dewey's approach to education or Jane Addams' Hull House are two examples particularly criticized in this context as creating a facade of concern for the individual while being ultimately manipulative themselves.)[27] A second solution that some of the individualists (e.g., Neil, Ferrer, and Leonard) propose is the development of schools in which all sorts of imposition and manipulation are avoided, and the emphasis is shifted from teaching to learning; from the transmission of ideas, contents, and values from adults to young people to the development of a child's ability to discuss, reveal, understand by himself. This approach, then, proposes the establishment of schools that safeguard and make prominent the individual and his powers.

The Socialist

The socialist critique is less of an attack on moral education per se than a criticism of moral education as generally practiced in contemporary bourgeois schools. The heart of this critique is that moral education constitutes one of the prominent devices of the capitalist order to subjugate the proletariat; that is, that schooling in capitalist societies (and particularly in America, which is the subject of much of this revisionist critique) is a carefully constructed device "to perpetuate already set patterns of social relationships of economic life and to facilitate integration of youth into the labor force."[28] According to this approach, the contents of schooling and the formal structure of schools, as well as the hidden curriculum and interpersonal relationships, reflect the unequalitarian, manipulative, and hierarchical power structure of the capitalist mentality.

This approach is critical of traditional schooling, progressive and other reform educational movements, and overly individualistic education.[29] The progressive education movement, for example, is seen as but "wrinkles on the brow" and as modifications of the basic capitalism that controls America ("the essence of Progressivism in education was the rationalization of the process of reproducing the social classes of modern industrial life.")[30] The free school philosophy of the 1960s is criticized for mislocating the core of the problem in the subjugation of the individual and in being naively individualistic.[31] This approach's inherent collectivism is in stark contrast to the radical individualism of the second critique.

The socialist critique calls for a radical restructuring of the entire social and economic order. What is needed is a recreation of society on the basis of an egalitarian ethic and under the control of the workers. In terms of education, this means the creation of schools that reflect and teach this new ethic. Thus, such schools would shift power to teachers, students, and local authorities; they would emphasize physical labor and work; they would teach the great values of socialism. In that sense, this critique is not against moral education per se, but rather against the particular ethic being taught. It would substitute the oppressive capitalist ethic with the more liberating socialist ethic. There is a second strain in this critique (e.g., Illich and Reimer) that proposes making available a host of educational resources for children and adults (networks of people, networks of things, libraries) that would help a person learn as he so desires. Such resources would be popularly accessible and available for use by the individual, rather than being superimposed on him/her.

The socialist critique of moral education then ultimately comes to replace a jaundiced morality with a more genuine and humane theory. It opposes moral education of the former order, but not of the latter.

Empirical Evaluative

The three arguments against moral education that we have examined so far have been rooted in ideological positions on the nature of knowledge, man, and society; that is, they reflect certain substantive philosophies of what *should* be. The fourth and fifth arguments are empirical rather than ideological; they doubt the validity of moral education on the basis of what they regard as empirical, sociological, and historical evidence. Thus, the empirical evaluative argument claims that research on moral education in schools over the years indicates that schooling is not a very important factor in affecting people's morality; hence, it concludes that the entire enterprise of attempting to carry out moral education in schools is a waste of time.

Such were the conclusions, according to Kohlberg, of the classic Hartshorne and May studies in character, which, he claims, resulted in a stagnation of the moral education enterprise in American education for decades.[32] While the Coleman and Jencks studies did not deal directly with moral education, they were similarly interpreted as critiques of the viability of schooling as compared with other factors (e.g., the socioeconomic level of the family) in affecting educational outcomes. This theme is echoed in popular critiques of suburban schooling, where supposedly the schools had little impact on young people's morality in regard to sex, drugs, and stealing.[33]

The conclusion drawn from such research and observation is that moral education, while perhaps a worthwhile activity, is simply not attainable in schools. There isn't enough time, teachers aren't adequately prepared, and there are too many outside pressures. Indeed, this argument is the inverse of our second and third arguments (the individualist and the socialist), which were critical of the great manipulative control schools have over children. This argument is more doubtful of the effects of schooling in the moral sphere. It claims that experience has shown morality to be too complex a phenomenon to be able to be taught or evaluated effectively in the span of a school year or a school setting; that is, it simply is too presumptuous to assume that schooling can affect morality.

The solution this approach offers to the dilemma is a retrenchment of the school's concern for the sphere of moral education, and instead, a concentration on those areas that schools can do well. Thus, the behavioral objectives movement aligns with this approach and emphasizes the teaching of contents, skills, and knowledge that can be clearly postulated, taught, and measured. Bereiter urges the two clearly defined and operational tasks of education: child care and skill training. Schools, according to this argument, should do what they are best equipped to do and not attempt to undertake impossible missions.

The Structural

The fifth claim against moral education has surfaced in other arguments; it is the contention that schools, by the very nature of their structure, have been proven to be institutions of manipulation and imposition. The individualist claim took the ideological position that schools thwart the crucial value of freedom; the socialist claim took the ideological position that schools would always be tools of elitism and against egalitarianism. The structural argument proposes to be an empirical observation about the *sui generis*, inherently manipulative nature of schools. This condition results from the fact that schools are separate institutions established by adults for the purpose of imposing some interest position on the young. The very nature of schooling educates for dependence on some outside force, whether theological, cultural, technological, socialist, or even anarchist.

Thus, Katz argues that "schools are designed to reflect and confirm the social structure that erected them,"[34] and in the case of American education, it means commitment to seven fundamental characteristics: (1) universal education, (2) tax-supported education, (3) free education, (4) compulsory education, (5) bureaucratic education, (6) racist education, and (7) class-biased education. Moreover, these fundamentals of American education are established and have remained constant for over one hundred years. Feinberg argues that "American schooling from kindergarten through graduate school operates to reinforce certain basic aspects of the American political, economic, and moral structure,"[35] and twentieth-century liberal educational policy is aimed at maintaining and adjusting that goal to shifting social and technological requirements.

Sociological analyses emphasize the following inherent aspects of school structure: the bureaucratic hierarchy, teacher authority in the classroom, seating procedures, sanctions and punishment, compulsory attendance, and examinations as tools of manipulation. Dreeben focuses on the contents and procedures utilized by American schools to transmit — beyond the formal curriculum — four key values of American life: independence, achievement, universalism, and specificity.[36] In a classic essay, Parsons focuses on the crucial educational effects of school and classroom structure.[37] The point made by the sociological analysis is that there is a decisive educative network over and above the formal curriculum, and it is in many ways a more prominent educator than the curriculum.

The structural argument, then, claims that the very establishment of schools as separate, specialized institutions and the doing of moral education therein implies the subjugation of the individual. Thus, unless we accept the authority of the imposing agency as legitimate (as is the case with Durkheim), then the entire operation of moral education in schools is unsatisfactory.

There are two solutions to this dilemma according to this argument: (1) the maximalist solution is the dissolution of schools and the return of education to the individual and the experiences of life (the Illich-Tolstoy argument); (2) the minimalist solution of the reduction of the tasks of schooling to only those areas that are free from any possibility of imposition (the Bereiter position). The former is preferable but near impossible to realize in modern society; the latter may be a bit easier to realize, but it is more susceptible of slipping into traditional moral education.

The Anti-Moral Education Tradition and Morality

The anti-moral education tradition encompasses the broad spectrum of views on the nature of morality that we find in classical and contemporary thought. Thus, some perspectives (e.g., Neil) see morality in exclusively individualistic terms, whereas the socialists start with social assumptions that are extremely close to Durkheim and Dewey. Tolstoy assumes the integral connection between religion and morality, whereas Ferrer disavows any such connection. Calvert's school is rooted in the assumption of the inherent connection between reason and morality, whereas Leonard emphasizes the personalist and mystical nature of experience. The socialists advocate teachers who can promulgate the socialist ethic, whereas Bereiter believes that the teacher's role is to develop basic skills and offer good care. Hence, there is no one underlying conception of morality in this school, and it reflects the broad spectrum of conceptions of morality that characterize the history of ethics and moral education.

Is there, then, enough in common to at all speak of the "anti-moral education school"? I think so, for the very position that schools should not engage in moral education constitutes a major dissent and break with a long-standing educational legacy. The question as to whether educational institutions have the right or responsibility to present, propose, teach, or impose a moral perspective is a major point of argument throughout the history of education. Those who reject schools' responsibility in this sphere may be odd bedfellows, but they are bedfellows. (Indeed, they probably are no more odd or diverse in view than those who affirm the function.)

Clearly, the anti-moral education movement has not become the dominant view and has usually remained the outsider, critic, or gadfly. This is so, first, because of the investment that society has made in the enterprise of education and moral education. To either dismantle or radically readjust schools as the anti-moral education movement has proposed would be to destroy one of the central political, economic, and ideological agencies of contemporary societies, and that is not something that societies would do very easily. A second reason for the outsider position of the anti-moral education movement is that it does not always offer clear alternatives to current practices of moral education or that the alternatives it does offer do not seem to be very much better. Some of the anti-moral education theories offer no alternatives at all to moral education; others propose an openness and non-directiveness that is either unclear or frightening to many parents and educators. Thus, the anti-moral education movement has frequently implied either overly ambiguous or overly radical pedagogic programs.

At the same time, the "anti" tradition has frequently been listened to and has not infrequently struck a responsive chord among school people, parents, and children. The message of manipulation, imposition, and loss of self is one that many teachers, parents, and children have experienced firsthand. While some of the pedagogic ideas proposed by moral educators have been successfully tried, there often is the nagging feeling that "more and more" moral education has not necessarily led to "more and more" morality. Thus, it is sometimes felt that maybe the "antis" are right, that the world would be in no worse shape without moral education—and that there would be far fewer uncomfortable examples of havoc wreaked by misguided moralities and moral education programs.

While the anti-moral education tradition has not succeeded in doing away with moral education, it has frequently had an impact on questioning and modifying standard approaches. In that sense, the anti-moral education movement must be considered one prominent category of twentieth-century moral education.

Chapter 7

DEWEY AND HIS FRIENDS TALK TOGETHER

WE HAVE BROUGHT TOGETHER in this volume some representative twentieth-century theories of morality and education. Our discussion has focused on a select group of particularly prominent and interesting theories, since it has not been possible to be all-inclusive. However, it is very clear that we could not complete a volume on moral education without discussion of some of John Dewey's perspectives on this topic. Much has been written by and about Dewey on moral education;[1] hence it is superfluous to present yet another summary of his views. However, the Deweyian perspective is of particular value as a focus for the comparison of the similarities and differences of the theories we have examined in detail. Hence, we invite Dewey and his approach to "chair" a summary discussion among the respective theories already discussed.

INDIVIDUAL AND SOCIAL

Three prominent conceptions of the relationship between the individual and the social in the moral sphere have surfaced in our discussion. One theory places the locus of emphasis on the individual. This approach, as voiced by VC and the individualistic strain of the anti-moral education school, regards moral development as part of the domain of individual confrontation and choice. According to this conception, genuine moral growth takes place within the individual, and it is best facilitated by the unimpeded development of the person. Accordingly, the task of moral education is neither to forge social being nor to develop social interaction; rather, it is to allow personal growth and prevent external imposition. Schools should help children to liberate themselves from forces of imposition and external control.

A second theory of the relationship between the individual and the social that has emerged in our discussions conceives of morality as a social phenomenon and moral education as social learning by the individual. According to such an approach, societies create morality and transmit it to their young through education; such transmission is not external imposition, but rather legitimate education, for without it morality would not exist. This approach is often associated with Durkheim, and his thinking does suggest some of these assumptions. As we shall see next, Durkheim is also aligned with another, different approach.

A third conception has emerged in our deliberation that casts doubt on the utility of the individual-social category for the analyses of morality and moral education.[2] Dewey, Kohlberg, and Durkheim represent an alternative theory of morality and moral development that proposes to reformulate the classic dualism between the individual and society, arguing that morality develops within the context of the interaction between individuals and social settings. Here are the voices of Dewey, Kohlberg, and Durkheim on the issue:

> The human being is an individual because of and in relation with others.[3]
>
> Man is a moral being only because he lives in society.[4]
>
> Morality is neither the internalization of established cultural values . . . nor the unfolding of spontaneous impulses and emotions, it is . . . the reciprocity between the individual and others in their social environment.[5]

(Can you tell which is which?) The interactionist thesis assumes that morality is a human experience defined by an integrative process between the two forces that the previous models attempted to isolate; hence, it rejects the viability of the reduction of morality to either one of these forces. Indeed, Dewey, Kohlberg, and Durkheim are critical of the very analytic prism that we have employed in this analysis.

Dewey's interactionism is strikingly typified by his seemingly modest volume, *Moral Principles in Education*. Much of this book attacks individualistic education and defends social-oriented education:

> The moral responsibility of the school, and of those who conduct it, is to society. The school is fundamentally an institution erected by society to do a certain, specific work — to exercise a certain specific function in maintaining the life and advancing the welfare of society.[6]
>
> Apart from participation in social life, the school has no moral end in mind.[7]

This does not seem to be the Dewey we thought we knew. Indeed, the Dewey of both *Experience and Education* and *Moral Principles in Education* simultaneously presents a personalist and a socialization theory of moral growth and education. *Moral Principles in Education* presents the thesis of moral being as the product of the dynamic interrelationship between self and social setting. According to this theory, morality cannot be reduced to one determinant factor, whether biological, psychological, or social. It is an emergent product of the interactive process.

While Durkheim, Kohlberg, and Dewey share this basic interactionist assumption, there also are significant factors that distinguish them from each other. Durkheim ascribes great significance to society's role in the interaction process and he treats society with much greater awe than either Kohlberg or Dewey. Consequently, Durkheim's practical program of moral education assigns greater influence to society in moral education than do Kohlberg or Dewey.

Dewey treats society with respect and regards it as a force of profound significance in human life and morality; at the same time, the emphasis is less on socialization into specific social norms and values and more on the development of the *process of interaction*. Dewey saw the school's role as mainly the development of the dynamic process of relationship between individual and society, rather than as the forging of specific social beings per se.

While Kohlberg constantly affirmed his interactionism, he was suspect in his early writings of being less concerned with interaction and more with individual (almost maturational) realization of Stage 6 justice. Later Kohlberg has been more faithful to his interactionist credo, as reflected both in his practical emphasis on the educative importance of the school community and more significantly in his increased attention to Stage 5 and 4 moralities. In all its versions, Kohlberg's theory does not reflect the Durkheimian awe of society; for him that reverence is reserved for justice.

John Wilson does not fit neatly into the three categories we have discussed. He shares the concern of Durkheim, Kohlberg, and Dewey for social dimensions of moral education; however, he is uncomfortable with the great power Durkheim ascribes to society in the moral sphere, and he does not share Dewey's and Kohlberg's emphasis on the process of interaction. Wilson affirms the classic dualism between the individual and society, and he proposes a utilitarian social contract theory of moral education that acknowledges the existence of the social and the need to make accommodations with it; at the same time, he affirms the integrity and uniqueness of the individual as a moral agent.

This topic has proven to be one of the important areas of debate in the philosophy of moral education, and it has serious implications for alternative practices of moral education. Three major spokesmen in our discussions constitute a uniquely twentieth-century attempt to present a new theoretical and practical conception of this topic.

MORAL PRINCIPLES

Moral principles and their role in education have proven to be a second controversial issue in the contemporary discussion of moral education. One prominent position that we have heard is a restatement of a distinguished philosophic tradition that focuses on the primacy of moral needs and habits rather than on principles; indeed, much of the practice of moral education seems to have followed this path. That tradition is represented in this volume by Durkheim's school, which focuses on a moral education concerned with the socialization of a person to certain norms and behaviors. Durkheim's version of the theory of moral socialization does not deny the existence of moral principles or of their place in moral education. However, they are not prior to or indispensable for the performance of moral behaviors or the acceptance of moral norms, and the thrust of the educational activity is to acculturate the child to understand and perform the *actions* implicit in moral principles.

Wilson, Kohlberg, and VC represent a second conception of moral principles and their role in moral education; this approach regards the moral principle as a primary and indispensable dimension of the moral sphere. Advocates of the "principled" notion of morality believe that to be moral means to choose a course of action on the basis of consideration of generalizable statements that reflect alternative value perspectives. To be moral is to think and choose in a principled way.

VC and some of the "antis" emphasize the nonobjective and pluralistic nature of moral principles in the twentieth century; their starting assumption is the crisis of the existence of alternative and nonverifiable sets of moral principles. Hence, they shift the focus of attention from values and principles themselves to the process of *deliberating* on and *choosing* values. In so doing, they deemphasize the role of moral principles, and instead greatly emphasize the choosing aspects of the process.

John Wilson and Lawrence Kohlberg also focus on the process of moral deliberation; however, they both pay great attention to the confrontation with moral principles as part of the moral process. Kohlberg and Wilson suggest that morality refers to deliberation and choice in terms of some universalizable, overriding value statement. For Kohlberg, justice is that universal principle which should directly affect the process of moral deliberation. While Wilson is not as explicit as Kohlberg in delineating the ultimate universal principle, his concept of PHIL does imply the role of overriding universalized principles in moral deliberation.[8] Thus, certainly Kohlberg (and very likely Wilson) believes that there is a specific, universalizable, moral principle that should affect the individual's moral deliberation. Both Wilson and Kohlberg are thoroughly committed to the notion that the process of moral deliberation based on principles is as crucial as the principle itself. Hence, principles should not be imposed on a person, but are to be confronted, wrestled with, and arrived at.

Dewey presents a conception of moral principles in education that differs from these two approaches and that in fact attempts to synthesize them. Dewey shares the assumption of the principled school that morality is minimally defined by the confrontation with and application of moral principles to value choices. He shares the belief in a notion of morality as choice of a course of action on the basis of some generalizable value statements.[9] Moreover, Dewey shares VC's picture of the modern age as characterized by the existence of a broad range of alternative value principles. However, he accepts neither Kohlberg's nor Wilson's assumption of some definitive universal moral principle nor VC's disregard of moral principles as central forces in the valuing process. Dewey, instead, conceives of moral principles as significant historical and social statements that have developed through experience and that are important and helpful referents for judging particular cases today.[10] While moral principles are not *a priori*, as Kohlberg argues, they certainly are significant statements about values that people have held and might want to hold. Moreover, Dewey suggests that there are some moral principles that seem to have proven themselves throughout time as particularly resilient and viable (e.g., democracy). Thus, the moral principle as a resource for consideration is a very central aspect of Dewey's theory.

Dewey is, then, certainly a charter member and founding father of the "principled school of moral education." However, his overall concern ultimately would seem to be to close the gap between the 'deed' and 'principled' schools. He is ultimately concerned with showing both Durkheim and VC that morality involves the choosing of deeds on the basis of principles. The polarization of their views constitutes for him a misrepresentation of the moral situation.

REASON IN ETHICS

Dewey cannot simply "chair" the discussion of this topic; he is such a central force in the affirmation of the role of reason in the twentieth-century theory of morality and moral education that we must first hear his own views.

There are five dimensions to the Deweyian conception of reason in ethics. First, reason is by nature practical, and its function is to affect practice. "The main role of philosophy is to deal with the 'problems of men,'"[11] and philosophy in this sense is for Dewey the essential operative force in life. (Scheffler suggests that Dewey's notion of philosophy as practical intelligence replaces for him the Hegelian notion of the Absolute Spirit.[12]) Second, reason is essentially one in all spheres; there is not a separate moral reasoning as opposed to other kinds of reasoning. The only difference between moral reasoning and other types of reasoning is the kind of topics thought about, but not the procedure or style of thinking.[13] Third, moral reasoning is a multifaceted process that involves: bumping into a problem, formulation of the problem, the collection of data and evidence, the development of a hypothesis or theory, and the testing of the theory.[14] These various steps are actually a dramatic or imaginative rehearsal of various courses of moral reasoning and conduct. Fourth, moral reasoning is not the opposite of either affect or habit. Dewey rejects the popular educational trilogy of cognitive, affective, and psychomotor, arguing instead that affect and habit are dimensions of moral reasoning.[15] Affect gives reflective morality the drive, passion, and concern that it needs to enable reasoning to move. Habit refers to systematic and dynamic behaviors rooted in thinking, which help us economize and operationalize moral reflection. Moral reasoning, in that sense, is all encompassing and multidimensional. Finally, reason in ethics is not determined by how much intelligence someone has, but by the will and ability to use reason in confronting ethical issues. Thus, reason in ethics is not measured by or reserved for scholars and noblemen; it is, like philosophy, a legacy for us all.

In general, almost all of the participants in this volume are of the cognitivist tradition in moral education represented by Dewey. They share his belief that morality should not be determined by collective authority, chance, or church; rather, they regard it as linked to reason and intelligence. While Wilson, VC, Kohlberg, and even Durkheim share the general commitment to the metaphor of 'reason in ethics', they understand this metaphor in different ways. Hence, Wilson, for example, shares the multidimensionality of moral reasoning of Dewey and the emphasis on morality as a process; however, Wilson regards moral reasoning as a distinct and unique category that cannot be assimilated into other forms of logic. Wilson's conception of moral reasoning is, moreover, more formal and less experimental than Dewey's. VC shares Dewey's emphasis on the procedural nature of thinking about values (i.e., 'valuing' rather than 'values') and on the integration of thinking, feeling, and action in the values sphere. However, for VC valuing is more concerned with personal expression and evocation and less with rigorous empirical or cognitive patterns than is the case for Dewey. Kohlberg shares Dewey's commitment to the practical nature of moral reasoning and to the unity of thinking, feeling, and behavior. However, his reasoning is less experimental and more deductive than Dewey's; for Kohlberg there is a built-in (formal) first principle of justice that significantly determines the reasoning process. Some anti-moral educationists — for example, Ferrer and Calvert — share Dewey's scientific model of moral reasoning; others — for example, Tolstoy or Illich — reject his attempt to assimilate moral reasoning in the model of scientific thinking. Durkheim argues that he too proposes a rational moral education, although his procedure of moral reasoning is more deductive and *a posteriori* than Dewey's, and it begins with conclusions rather than arrives at them.

Despite these differences, Dewey certainly feels more at home in the schools of Durkheim, Wilson, VC, and Kohlberg than he does at other schools on the block. The schools of moral education represented in this volume constitute one major contemporary approach that is centrally committed to the belief that reason is an indispensable component of ethics and education for morality.

FORM AND CONTENT

Many of our "guests" reveal a particularly fighting spirit when it comes to this topic; and they are very much concerned to argue that morality does not refer to specific norms, principles, or dos and don'ts, but rather to styles or procedures of confronting moral problems. VC presents this conception most vividly in its contention that values education refers to the teaching of the process of valuing, rather than to the teaching of specific values. Kohlberg and Wilson also demonstratively assert their commitment to a formal rather than substantive notion of morality.

While some of the representatives of this "process" school cite Dewey as their father, he denies patrimony on this issue. The main thrust of Dewey's comments on this topic is once again to doubt the very utility of the form-content category. Dewey proposes that the alleged dualism of form and content is fictitious, and that morality, in fact, is a unity of the two. This unity is most vividly expressed in Dewey's theory of moral habit as a dynamic activity encompassing both repetitious practical behavior as well as the potential for adaptation and adjustment.[16] To be moral, says Dewey, is both to apply a procedure and to accept or operationalize some contents (just as to "have an experience" refers both to the process someone undergoes as well as to the content or event undergone).

It is often suggested that whereas Kohlberg, VC, and Wilson are process oriented, and Dewey is concerned with the interaction of process and content, Durkheim is a classic example of a theory of morality as content. He certainly does focus directly on content dimensions of morality; at the same time, our interpretation of Durkheim places him closer to the Dewey-ian perspective than is usually thought. Durkheim presents a notion of morality as content *reflective of the autonomous sense.* Morality is not just content for him, it is also a point of view and a "sense." It is instructive for us that Durkheim's exemplars of moral excellence are, as Kohlberg's, from the prophetic rather than priestly tradition. Jesus and Socrates are moral models for Durkheim both because of their behaviors and deeds and also because they represent an approach or a perspective to all spheres of life that can be characterized as 'moral'.

Why have theorists of education been so persistent in arguing for a notion of morality as form? First, some of them have been influenced by major trends in twentieth-century moral philosophy in which the search for a formalist philosophy has been prominent.[17] Second, they are reacting to the great emphasis that the practice of education has placed on morality as content. Many theorists have been concerned with what they regard as a corrupted view of morality as specific behaviors rather than as a style of thinking.

Once again, in our discussion, we see how John Dewey assumes the role of great mediator and synthesizer between what he regards as mischievous philosophic and educational polarizations.

ACTION

Dewey is pleased with the almost unanimous commitment to action as a factor in the moral sphere that has echoed throughout this book. Our "guests" share the belief that 'being moral' is only fully realized and defined when it is expressed in some practical action or deed.

The major question of our theorists has not been whether action is important to morality, but whether schools should teach specific actions. Several of our approaches seem to deemphasize the teaching of specific actions. Thus, VC places little emphasis on the teaching of specific deeds and much more on the process of choosing and/or on deeds chosen. Wilson also is very much concerned with a person's ability to employ the moral components to deal with a moral problem; thus, while he has periodically suggested specific courses on morality, his concern has been with the teaching of a process of moral deliberation based on the moral components, rather than with the teaching of specific behaviors. Early Kohlberg was accused of deemphasizing education for moral action at the expense of moral judgment. Durkheim, of course, is not included in such a charge, since he openly advocates a system that could develop very specific deeds and actions; at the same time, it is interesting that we do not find a detailed list or curriculum of deeds and actions in Durkheim's writings on moral education. Indeed, he does *not* present a practical program of specific moral deeds to be taught to children.

Dewey adds two clarifications to this discussion. First, he suggests that one of the ways that one teaches the process of morality is via specific deeds. His entire theory of education is based on a conception of education that rejects the possibility of teaching a process without actual experiences or deeds and that simultaneously rejects the value of experiences that do not have a reflective, growth dimension.

Second, Dewey suggests that most of our theorists have neglected two concepts that are crucial to the sphere of moral action: moral habit and moral passion.[18] Moral action does not exist in itself; it is motivated and charged by moral passion and it is regularized by and channeled into moral habits. Some of our guests deal with one or the other of these items (e.g., Wilson — passion; Durkheim — habits), but most do not weave both together into an overall theory of moral education.

The emphasis on judgment, reflection, and intention that emerges in our theories has led some critics to argue that twentieth-century schools of moral education have neglected education for moral action. Our discussion reveals the inaccuracy of that charge. The proceduralists do not come to do away with action as a concern of moral education, but to propose a new approach for bringing about moral actions.

THE MORALLY EDUCATED PERSON

One of the great contributions of our guests is the presentation in remarkable detail of the characteristics of people whom they regard as morally educated. Dewey too presents such a list of characteristics, and it proves to be a useful yardstick against which to compare our other theories.[19]

First, Dewey's moral person reflects on and reasons about moral issues, according to a clearly delineated process of thinking (problem/information/hypothesis and theory/testing/conclusion). Second, such a person confronts moral issues with moral feeling and passion (which sometimes has been referred to as 'conscience'). This means that the moral person expresses great concern, interest, and excitement about the issue in question and its outcome. Third, the morally educated person is part of a social group and community and is informed by them. He/she does not exist in a vacuum but is affected by (and affects) a group. Hence, the morally educated person has social concerns, responsibilities, and skills. Fourth, the morally educated person has developed certain habits or dispositions that are expressed in his/her daily life. These habits are adaptable and they reflect moral reasoning, but they nonetheless do function as a part of the personality and daily life-style of the person.

Finally, the morally educated person is a 'total' or 'organic' self (an idea sometimes associated with the concept of 'character') in the sense that his/her thoughts and action in daily life reflect some consistent and comprehensible pattern, rather than a haphazard or inconsistent series of moral responses. The morally educated person responds to the many ongoing experiences of life in a manner that reflects some overall and reflected-upon pattern or world view.[20]

Durkheim's model of the morally educated person encompasses four of the Deweyian components (duty = passion and habit, community = community; autonomy = reflection): it does not include the concept of the total self; moreover, Durkheim's notion of reasoning is different from Dewey's. Wilson's moral components share Dewey's commitment to reflection (KRAT) and moral feeling (PHIL), but do not emphasize community or the organic self to the same extent as Dewey. VC continues the Deweyian motifs of the organic self and moral feelings, but neglects his emphasis on habit, community, and reflection. Kohlberg shares the Deweyian emphasis on reflection, the organic self, and, (increasingly) community, but not moral passion ("conscience") or habit.

Dewey's treatment of the morally educated person underscores three themes that have surfaced throughout this book. First, our theorists generally point to the interrelationship between moral self and development and general self and development, and they usually do not deal with the moral being and education of the child in total isolation from his/her other "education" or development. Thus, it is no accident that VC, Kohlberg, Wilson, and Dewey write about moral education in the context of other forms and issues of education and interpersonal intervention (e.g., humanistic education, religious education, education of the emotions, education in prisons, and mental health). Their morally educated people are educated both morally and otherwise, and for most of our theorists morality is one of the active and interactive domains of human existence.

Second, several of our theories focus on the multidimensionality of morality, that is, the fact that the moral person encompasses several traits, abilities, dispositions, and skills. This, of course, implies a multidimensional conception of moral education as being concerned with the development and integration of these several qualities in children. This multidimensionality is an idea that the practice of moral education has found most difficult to accept and operationalize; and schools continue to look for that *one* trait or characteristic that defines 'morality'. Most of our theorists are saying to the world of practice that the search for the one trait is a futile and misleading activity.

Third, most of our theorists (with the exception of some of the anti-moral educationists) subscribe to the belief that the qualities of the morally educated person can in some way be affected by and developed through schooling. Most of our friends believe that intentional, thoughtful planning and intervention in schools can contribute to the development of some or all of these moral components in children. Our theorists see this intervention as an ongoing process to be effected over time and not easily measurable at short range; but they do believe that over an extended time span we can talk about — and hence should plan for — the role of schooling in the development of the morally educated person.

INDOCTRINATION

R. S. Peters has suggested that the analysis of 'indoctrination' has been one of the unique contributions of contemporary British philosophy of education.[21] It is not a concept that has been dealt with systematically or in the same fashion by all our guests; some have directly analyzed it, while others have only dealt with it in passing or by implication. Indeed, Dewey finds it somewhat complicated to chair this part of the summary, for he too feels that some of the relevant terms of reference are not part of his own analysis. As Willis Moore suggests, "The current argument among our British colleagues as to whether 'indoctrination' should be defined in terms of aim, content or method or some combination of these, could hardly occur in the context of contemporary [American] philosophy of education."[22]

Nevertheless, there are some emergent patterns in the various discussions of this concept. Those of our guests who use the term imply by it some illegitimate or distasteful activity. 'Indoctrination' clearly functions as an emotive educational concept in our discussion to connote an activity that is regarded as nondesirable. Usually, 'indoctrination' is contrasted with the (positive) term 'education', which refers to the particular normative theory being advocated. Hence, one characteristic that the concept 'indoctrination' has in common in all its uses among our guests is its negative connotation.

When we come to analyze the substance of the various notions of 'indoctrination', the emergent conceptions do, in fact, deviate according to the categories of content, method, and aim.[23] For Kohlberg, Ferrer, Calvert, and others in the anti-moral education school, 'indoctrination' refers to the imposition of certain kinds of contents (or doctrines) that are nonobjective, not agreed upon, and/or not verifiable. For Ferrer, to teach the Gospels or church theology is to indoctrinate, because it is to transmit contents whose veracity is in doubt or not agreed upon. Adherents of this school do not oppose the act of imposition per se; indeed, they affirm the legitimacy of teaching contents that are true and verifiable. Thus, Kohlberg affirms the concept of 'justice' since it is a natural fact. Ferrer affirms the right and responsibility to teach scientific methods, and Durkheim affirms the need to transmit social facts in order to perpetuate morality. Consequently this group sees 'indoctrination' as linked to the transmission of questionable contents.

A second group of thinkers has accepted Hare's position that 'indoctrination' does not refer to questionable or unquestionable contents (indeed, there is a great deal of question about what makes a content questionable or not!), but rather to the aim or intention of the educator vis à vis any contents. If the aim is to predetermine or program a student's judgment about issues, then such an activity is 'indoctrination'; if the aim of the educator is to provide students with the tools and the rational abilities to consider matters and arrive at their own decisions, then the activity is 'education'. VC and (later) Wilson represent this concern with developing children's abilities to judge matters on their own; and VC particularly is vehement in its rejection of any procedures that suggest the slightest possibility of imposition. In this way, VC emphasizes certain types of open teaching methods as opposed to authoritarian pedagogic procedures. Hence, it is not because methods per se define 'indoctrination', but because open methods reflect the nonjudgmental aim, whereas authoritarian methods reflect the concern with imposition; however, it is not the method alone that defines 'indoctrination'.

While the terminology used in this discussion is not Deweyian, the problem being discussed is clearly known to him.[24] Dewey follows the general pattern of regarding 'indoctrination' as an undesirable activity which is opposed to 'education'. 'Education' for Dewey refers to the aim and attempt to advance growth; mis-education or 'indoctrination' would refer to activities whose intent and/or effect is to thwart growth. 'Indoctrination' is not defined by specific methods or by specific contents, just as education is not characterized by specific methods or contents. What characterizes education for Dewey is the dynamic relationship between a student and contents and experiences — where the intention is to help the student in his/her ability to further growth; indoctrination is about the application of techniques in relation to certain contents or experiences that come to thwart such growth.

Are moral, religious, and political education regarded as the paradigms of 'indoctrination' according to our theorists? While reservations about classical religious, political, and moral education do surface in our discussion, our theorists do not regard these activities as *sui generis* paradigms of 'indoctrination'. Rather, their position is that there often have been excesses in these three spheres that have turned 'education' into 'indoctrination'; however, this pattern is historical and sociological and not logical. Indeed, several of our guests (e.g., Dewey, Kohlberg, and Wilson) are sympathetic to moral, religious, and political approaches as types of schooling that deal with the "great" issues of life. Thus, the ultimate concern of most of our theorists seems paradoxically to show that (1) moral, religious, and political education are not per se indoctrinary and (2) they encompass the most important and basic concerns of education. Indeed, our guests seem to be suggesting that the issues that moral, political, and religious education deal with are among the most important and essential concerns of education.

THE TEACHER

The teachers, the poor teachers! They are bombarded with orders, suggestions, directives, and theories as to how to improve their efforts and save the world. The ills of education are placed on the doorsteps of the teachers, who are expected to assume responsibility for the speedy creation of a better age.

Our guests have proven to be very genuinely and realistically concerned with the tasks of teachers in moral education. Most of our theorists have spent a good deal of time with teachers, and they have come to understand their situation and sympathize with their tasks. Consequently, what emerges are some clear and quite practical directives for teachers' roles in moral education.

We find three distinct models of the role of the teacher in moral education in our discussion. The first model is Durkheim's conception of the teacher as transmitter of the great values of a particular society. In this case, the teacher's role is to represent and transmit those values that a society holds dear. This model conceives of the teacher as a servant or priest of society whose behaviors and teaching should honorably represent society's norms. At the same time, Durkheim does not propose to turn the teacher into a robot. He is sensitive to the human complexities of being a representative of society's values; moreover, he believes that the school should help students to reflect upon and even react to society's values. Thus, despite the admittedly exemplary and definitive role apparently ascribed to the teacher by Durkheim (epitomized in his metaphor of the teacher as hypnotist), his writings also reveal a concern with the reflective aspects of the life of the teacher in the classroom.

The second model of teacher is as therapist or facilitator. This model is best represented by VC, and it regards the teacher's role as one of helping students to relate personally and emotionally to moral issues. The qualities demanded of the teacher in this case focus less on behavioral and intellectual skills than Durkheim does; rather, they encompass the interpersonal and intrapersonal ability to stimulate reflection and expression. Such a teacher is not society's priest or its prophet, but its therapist.

The third model regards the teacher as pedagogue of the process of moral deliberation or moral judgment. According to this model, the teacher's ultimate goal is to develop in children that process of judgment or deliberation, which constitutes the essence of morality. Hence, teachers do not come to develop specific behaviors or to represent specific norms; nor is their role exclusively to stimulate discussion or encourage self-expression. Rather, the teacher comes to transmit, stimulate, and develop a specific process. In contradistinction to the second model, this model ascribes a specific substance to the teacher's role; however, the substance is not specific norms or behaviors, but rather a generalized moral process. Thus, the teacher should be knowledgeable in the process (whether it be Wilson's moral components or Kohlberg's moral judgment) and skilled in pedagogic procedures of developing this process in children.

Dewey's approach to the teacher in moral education combines the first and third categories, and reflects his larger conception of the two-fold role of the teacher in education: (1) the social role and (2) the growth function. Dewey sees the teacher as a part of society, as its agent, and as very much responsible to and reflective of society. Thus, in his summary chapter to the first publication of the newly formed John Dewey Society (1937), Dewey begins his analysis of the nature of teachers by stressing their crucial role in the fight against fascism:

> In earlier chapters we have seen how classroom methods, teacher attitudes, community activities, school administration, and teacher organizations can play a part in the struggle to advance the democratic ideal in defiance of any threat of fascism. But there can be no certainty of victory. . . . The teacher must be deeply and passionately concerned with this great historic choice.[25]

The language and content of this passage is very much that of the model of the teacher as exemplar and advocate of a society's loftiest values.

The second function of the teacher according to Dewey is as "a student of child development, a friendly guide to individual children, an organizer of harmonious group activities, and a "generalist" in thinking about the effects of the social order upon personal growth."[26] This function of the teacher refers to his/her ability to organize and integrate worthwhile activities for the developing personality. Such a task is aimed at enabling the child to wholly and personally experience an activity; to enable an experience to become part of a person's being. Hence, the teacher should be concerned, not with the subject matter as such, but with the subject matter as a factor in a total and growing experience. This second function then focuses on the organization of setting, procedure, and materials, which will help the child learn how to experience.

The nonfrontal and flexible dimension of this second function has sometimes led people to regard Dewey's teacher as of the therapist model; in fact, however, this is not the case. Dewey's teacher comes to represent certain values of a society and to stimulate and develop certain processes in children; that is, Dewey's teacher combines models one and three and argues against model two.

Many of the writings of the theorists we have examined in this volume reflect a discomfort with conceptions of the teacher as an omnipotent, omniscient source of truth for children, and consequently, there is a search for less authoritative role definitions. At the same time, most of our guests are not willing to abandon totally the teacher's priestly or prophetic function and to accept VC's radical model of the neutral teacher. Thus, Wilson wants his teacher to be a moral philosopher; Kohlberg wants his teacher to be Jesus, Socrates, or Korczak, and Dewey wants the teacher to be integrator of experience and warrior against fascism. While some of our thinkers are wary of the weight of the garments of the classical priest, they are not willing to discard totally this garb. For most of our thinkers, teaching remains very much an essentially moral activity.

PEDAGOGY

Finally, we come to the classroom; the long road of analysis of some major contemporary theories of moral education ends where education begins – in the classroom.

Three motifs emerge in our discussion of the pedagogy of moral education. Most of our theories take seriously the function of the classroom and the role of teaching in the classroom as a dimension of moral education, although they differ in their conceptions of the content or 'subject' of morality to be taught there. Thus, Wilson, Kohlberg, and Dewey regard the process of moral deliberation as the content of moral education. Durkheim regards moral norms and behaviors as the legitimate contents of moral education. VC theorists regard the process of valuing as the content. The bulk of these theorists shift the emphasis away from specific norms and dictates; even Durkheim who is a champion of specific norms does not stipulate a specific code or curriculum of norms and dictates.

Thus, with the exception of some of the anti-moral educationists, most of our theorists assume that morality can be curricularized in schools, albeit not as a "conventional subject."

A second motif that surfaces in several of our theories is the role of the informal, hidden, or extracurriculum in moral education. Durkheim and Dewey emphasize the role of the school as a community for moral education; later Kohlberg focuses on the 'just community' school or participatory democracy as a vehicle for moral education, and Wilson suggests the value of the boarding school model as a positive form for moral education. Clearly, even apparently cognitive and analytic models of moral education are not willing to dispense with other parallel and perhaps no less insignificant avenues of "doing" moral education.

A third motif that appears in all of our theories except Durkheim's is the primacy of the child as an agent in his/her own moral development. Some theories (Wilson, Kohlberg) present carefully constructed Socratic dialogues to involve the learner in a precisely delineated thinking process. VC supporters propose a provocative set of questions and procedures aimed at opening up the child's value reflections. Dewey proposes a set of educational experiences that will flow from the child's interest and involvement. These theories assume a learning theory that necessitates learner initiative and participation. Durkheim presents an alternative model that is not dependent on an interest theory and that even assumes an initial tension between learner and contents; such tension is in fact a creative force and source of moral growth.

All of our theories share in common a commitment to the importance of pedagogy as an aspect of the discussion of moral education. Some present very practical proposals, projects, and procedures for doing moral education while others present general guidelines. All share a commitment to somehow translating moral theory into some operative educational practice.

CONCLUSION

I have avoided the temptation to make an overly neat comparative taxonomy of the theories that we have explored. The Dewey prism shows us that there are all sorts of interconnections, comparisons, and surprising similarities and differences among our theories. VC, Kohlberg, and some of the anti-moral educationists claim direct lineage to Dewey; yet these children do not always look like their father, and rarely do they look like each other. Kohlberg and VC are of the same period and educational milieu, yet their approaches reflect strikingly different diagnoses and prescriptions. Dewey and Durkheim lived on different continents and reflected different intellectual traditions, yet their views often prove to be strikingly similar. Thus, rather than constructing neat boxes and charts in this chapter, we have been concerned with suggesting and pursuing possible similarities, connections, and differences.

Our analysis does, indeed, reveal some basic differences of opinion among twentieth-century schools of moral education on key issues related to morality and education. However, our discussion suggests that an even more significant disagreement may exist between the common motifs of *theories* of moral education and what actually happens in *schools*. There are, in particular, three motifs that have emerged as central to most of the theories of moral education examined in this book that constitute pedagogic problems for moral educational practice: (1) the multidimensionality of morality, (2) the role of reason in ethics, and (3) morality as a principled activity. Schools have dealt with the translation into educational practice of other dimensions of the moral sphere that have emerged in this volume, for example, moral passion, moral habits, and moral norms. Our theories suggest that the activity of moral education is incomplete unless it also encompasses the factors of moral complexity, moral reasoning, and moral principles. The translation of these philosophic factors into practical educational strategies and programs is, admittedly, a most complex procedure and a joint enterprise for philosophy and education. Indeed, some of our theories constitute attempts to begin this process.

This task is not solely academic; the moral failures of the twentieth century and the moral wrestlings of the contemporary young person clearly indicate that the issues of moral education are far from being resolved. Dewey and his friends have attempted to help us reflect on these issues in the hope of better introducing our young to the mysteries and majesty of the moral sphere. If we have learned anything from our teachers it is that now is the time for us to come and reason together.

NOTES
BIBLIOGRAPHY
INDEX

NOTES

PREFACE

1. Recent developments and publications in the area of moral education are recorded in the journal Moral Education Forum. Two comprehensive resources for existing materials in the field up to the mid-1970s are Douglas Superka, "A Typology of Valuing Theories and Values Education Approaches" (Ph.D. diss., School of Education, University of California, Berkeley, 1973); Douglas Superka, Christine Ahrens, Judith Hedstrom, Luther Ford, and Patricia Johnson, eds., Values Education Sourcebook: Conceptual Approaches, Materials Analyses, and an Annotated Bibliography (Boulder, Colo.: Social Science Education Consortium, 1976).
2. Barry Chazan and Jonas Soltis, eds., Moral Education (New York: Teachers College Press, 1973).

CHAPTER 1. THE ISSUES OF MORAL EDUCATION

1. See the following for some helpful introductory comments about the key issues of moral philosophy: William Frankena, Ethics, 2d ed. (Englewood Cliffs, N.J.: Prentice-Hall, 1973); William Frankena, Thinking About Morality (Ann Arbor: University of Michigan Press, 1980); Robert Nozick, Philosophical Explanations (Cambridge, Mass.: Harvard University Press, 1981). One of the best introductions to the issues and history of moral philosophy is John Dewey with James Hayden Tufts, Ethics (New York: Henry Holt, 1908).
2. John Dewey, Human Nature and Conduct (New York: Modern Library, 1922). P. W. Musgrave, The Moral Curriculum: A Sociological Analysis (London: Methuen, 1978).
3. Marcus Singer, Generalization in Ethics (New York: Knopf, 1961).
4. For a recent example of such a substantive discussion, see G. J. Warnock, The Object of Morality (London: Methuen, 1971). See also the following discussion of Warnock and other related issues: Brian Crittendon, Bearings in Moral Education (Hawthorn, Victoria, Australia: Australian Council for Educational Research, 1978).
5. R. M. Hare, "Language and Moral Education," in The Domain of Moral Education, P. B. Cochrane, C. M.

Hamm, and A. C. Kazepides, eds. (New York and Toronto: Paulist Press and Ontario Institute for Studies in Education, 1979), pp. 89-106.

6. One of the classic volumes on this subject is Stephen Toulmin, An Examination of the Place of Reason in Ethics (Cambridge: Cambridge University Press, 1960).

7. See the following discussion of these schools: Mary Warnock, Ethics Since 1900 (London: Oxford University Press, 1960).

8. R. M. Hare, The Language of Morals (New York: Oxford University Press, 1964). See also Barry Chazan, "The Moral Situation: Prolegomenon to Moral Education," in Moral Education, Chazan and Soltis, eds., pp. 39-49.

9. William Frankena, "Toward a Philosophy of Moral Education," Harvard Educational Review, XXVIII (Fall 1958), pp. 303-313; reprinted in Moral Education, Chazan and Soltis, eds., pp. 148-158.

10. Frankena, "Toward a Philosophy of Moral Education."

11. R. S. Peters, "Reason and Habit: The Paradox of Moral Education," in Moral Education in a Changing Society, W. R. Niblett, ed. (London: Faber and Faber, 1963), pp. 46-65. See also R. S. Peters, Ethics and Education (London: Allen and Unwin, 1961).

12. R. M. Hare, The Language of Morals, pp. 74-78; reprinted in Moral Education, Chazan and Soltis, eds., pp. 99-102.

13. P. B. Cochrane, "Prolegomena to Moral Education," in The Domain of Moral Education, pp. 73-88. See also Andrew Oldenquist, "Moral Education Without Moral Education: Review Essay," Harvard Educational Review, XLIX, 2 (May 1979), pp. 240-247.

14. See the following discussions of this issue: Harry Broudy, Michael J. Parsons, Ivan A. Snook, Ronald D. Szoke, Philosophy of Education: An Organization of Topics and Selected Sources (Urbana: University of Illinois Press, 1967); Leslie Stevenson, Seven Theories of Human Nature (New York: Oxford University Press, 1974).

15. See the following detailed analyses of issues related to sex bias in conceptions of the "ideal person" and in philosophy of education generally: Jane Roland Martin, "Sophie and Emile: A Case Study of Sex Bias in the History of Educational Thought," Harvard Educational Review, LI, 3 (August 1981), pp. 357-372; Jane Roland Martin, "Excluding Women from the Educational Realm," Harvard Educational Review, LII, 2 (May 1983), pp. 133-148; Jane Roland Martin, "The Ideal of the Educated Person," Educational Theory, XXXI, 2 (Spring 1981), pp. 97-109.

16. Much of this literature is collected and discussed in the following two volumes: I. A. Snook, ed., Concepts of Indoctrination (London: Routledge and Kegan Paul, 1972); I. A. Snook, Indoctrination and Education (London: Routledge and Kegan Paul, 1972).

CHAPTER 2. EMILE DURKHEIM: MORAL
EDUCATION AS MORAL SOCIALIZATION

1. Emile Durkheim, Moral Education (New York: Free Press, 1961), pp. 59-60.

2. Emile Durkheim, "The Determination of Moral Facts," Sociology and Philosophy (Glencoe, Ill.: Free Press, 1953), p. 37.

3. Ibid., p. 50.

4. Emile Durkheim, The Division of Labor in Society (New York: Macmillan, 1933), p. 399.

5. Durkheim, "The Determination of Moral Facts," p. 52.

6. Emile Durkheim, "The Dualism of Human Nature and Its Social Conditions," in Emile Durkheim, Kurt H. Wolff, ed. (Columbus: Ohio State University Press, 1960); Durkheim, "The Determination of Moral Facts," pp. 44-45. See also the following discussion of Durkheim on this issue: Steven Lukes, Emile Durkheim, His Life and Work: A Historical and Critical Study (New York: Penguin Books, 1973), pp. 412-414; Ernest Wallwork, Durkheim: Morality and Milieu (Cambridge, Mass.: Harvard University Press, 1972), p. 157.

7. For a discussion of two senses of 'morality', one individual and one social, see John Wilson, Norman Williams, and Barry Sugarman, Introduction to Moral Education (Harmondsworth, Eng.: Penguin Books, 1967), pp. 44-45.

8. Emile Durkheim, "Education: Its Nature and Role," Education and Sociology (New York: Free Press, 1956), p. 70.

9. Pickering argues that in denying the very existence of this dichotomy, Durkheim is never able to have a positive conception of the individual:

> Durkheim, it might be said, was never able to solve the dichotomy between the individual and the social . . . . By virtually equating the moral with the social, linked by the notion of duty, the person or individual is either disregarded or underplayed . . . . The 'individual' component does not have a place of any significance.

His argument, in fact, neglects Durkheim's theory of the dual nature of man: W. S. F. Pickering, "Introduction to Part I (Morals)," in Durkheim: Essays on Morals and Education, W. S. F. Pickering, ed. (London: Routledge and Kegan Paul, 1979), p. 12.

10. See the following discussions of this motif in Durkheim's social theory: Robert Nisbet, The Sociology of Emile Durkheim (New York: Oxford University Press, 1974), p. 33; Robert Bellah, "Introduction," in Emile Durkheim on Morality and Society, Robert Bellah, ed. (Chicago: University of Chicago Press, 1973), pp. ix-xv.

11. Durkheim, "Education: Its Nature and Role" and "Pedagogy and Sociology," Education and Sociology, pp. 72-73 and p. 124.

12. Durkheim, "The Dualism of Human Nature and Its Social Conditions," p. 151.

13. Durkheim, "Education: Its Nature and Role," p. 72.

14. Durkheim, Moral Education, p. 92.

15. Emile Durkheim, Suicide: A Study in Sociology (Glencoe, Ill.: Free Press, 1952).

16. Robert Nisbet, The Sociology of Emile Durkheim, p. 118.

17. Lukes, Emile Durkheim, His Life and Work, pp. 433-434.

Durkheim deepened and extended that hypothesis, towards the end of his life, in a way that is sharply reminiscent of the thought of the later Freud (see note 27). He argued that . . .
there is in man a permanent tension between the demands of social life and those of his individual, organic nature, a tension which will increase with the advance of civilization. (p. 433)

18. Durkheim, "The Dualism of Human Nature and Its Social Conditions," pp. 102-103. See Sigmund Freud, Civilization and Its Discontents (New York: W. W. Norton, 1961), pp. 90-91.

19. Durkheim, "The Determination of Moral Facts," pp. 63-80.

20. Ibid., pp. 64-65.

21. Ibid., p. 38.

22. Wallwork, Durkheim: Morality and Milieu, pp. 1-2.

23. There is a sense in which the use of the phrase 'moral principles' in the context of an analysis of Durkheim's theory of morality is misleading and, in fact, foreign to Durkheim's system. I have utilized the phrase for two reasons: (1) it is prominent in some of the other approaches to be examined in this book, especially Kohlberg and Wilson, and I am interested in categories relevant to several approaches so as to enable comparisons; (2) Durkheim ultimately does deal with many underlying issues implied by the phrase 'moral principles', even if he does not normally use the phrase itself.

24. These questions are dealt with by Durkheim in "The Determination of Moral Facts," and in "Introduction à la morale," Revue Philosophique, LXXXIX, pp. 79-87; translated as "Introduction to Ethics," in Durkheim: Essays on Morals and Education, pp. 77-96. This apparently was the last work written by Durkheim before his death on November 15, 1916 (see Lukes, Emile Durkheim, His Life and Work, pp. 558-559).

25. The following discussion claims that Durkheim defined 'moral facts' in several different ways: J. Henriot, part 2, chapter 1 in Existence et obligation (Paris: P. U. F., 1967).

26. Durkheim, "Introduction to Ethics," p. 89.

27. W. S. F. Pickering, "Introduction to Part I (Morals)," p. 10. See also Emile Durkheim, chapter 1 in The Rules of Sociological Method (Glencoe, Ill.: Free Press, 1950).

28. In "The Determination of Moral Facts," Durkheim
uses the terms 'morality' and 'moral facts' interchange-
ably.
29. Emile Durkheim, "Contribution to 'Morality Without God: An Attempt to Find a Collectivist Solution,'" in
Durkheim: Essays on Morals and Education, p. 34.
30. Durkheim, "The Determination of Moral Facts,"
p. 35.
31. Ibid., p. 36.
32. Ibid.
33. Durkheim specifically refers to his approach in
terms of the Kantian and utilitarian systems in his lecture on "Value Judgments and Judgments of Reality" to the
International Congress of Philosophy, April 6, 1911,
later published in Revue de Métaphysique et de Morale
(July 3, 1911) and in Durkheim, Sociology and Philosophy,
pp. 87-95.
34. Durkheim, Sociology and Philosophy, pp. 86-93.
See also Durkheim, "Introduction to Ethics," p. 81. One
of the issues debated by Durkheim scholars is whether or
not his thought vis à vis moral ideals underwent major
shifts toward the latter part of his life. Some have
argued that there were major shifts in his position (e.g.,
Wallwork), whereas others point to a constant theme with
changing emphases. See Talcott Parsons, The Structure of
Social Action (Glencoe, Ill.: Free Press, 1949); G. Davy,
"Durkheim: II--l'oeuvre," Revue de Métaphysique et de
Morale, XXVII, pp. 71-112; Lukes, "The Sociology of
Morality," chapter 21 in Emile Durkheim, His Life and Work;
Wallwork, "Ethical Theory," chapter 6 in Durkheim: Morality and Milieu; Mark Traugott, "Introduction," in Emile
Durkheim on Institutional Analysis, Mark Traugott, ed.
(Chicago: University of Chicago Press, 1978); Pickering,
"Introduction to Part I (Morals)," pp. 21-26.
35. Durkheim, "Introduction to Ethics," p. 81.
36. Durkheim, "Value Judgments and Judgments of
Reality," p. 93.
37. Durkheim, "Introduction to Ethics," p. 92.
38. Ibid.
39. This concern with moral ideals is especially
evident in Moral Education, which is regarded as a late
and more sophisticated formulation of Durkheim's moral
stance and the fragmentary "Introduction a la Morale"
("Introduction to Ethics").
40. This is the interpretation given by Madhu Suri
Prakash to Bellah's essay on the uniqueness of Durkheim's
secular morality. See Robert Bellah, "Introduction,"
p. ix; Madhu Suri Prakash, "Moral Education and the Initiation Into the Institution of Morality," Philosophy of
Education, 1981, Daniel R. De Nicola, ed. (Normal, Ill.:
Philosophy of Education Society, 1982), pp. 105-114.
41. Wallwork, Durkheim: Morality and Milieu, p. 9.
42. Durkheim, Moral Education, p. 120.
43. Durkheim, The Rules of Sociological Method
pp. xxxix-xl; Durkheim, Moral Education, pp. 4 and 265:
"The rationalist postulate may be stated thus: there is

nothing in morality that one is justified in considering
as fundamentally beyond the scope of human reason"
(p. 4). See also: P. Q. Hirst, Durkheim, Bernard, and
Epistemology (London: Routledge and Kegan Paul, 1975),
pp. 81-115.
    44. Emile Durkheim, The Evolution of Educational
Thought (London: Routledge and Kegan Paul, 1977).
    45. Wallwork, Durkheim: Morality and Milieu, pp. 35-
37.
    46. Durkheim, "Introduction à la Morale," p. 92.
    47. Durkheim, Moral Education, p. 120. See the sec-
tion entitled "The Morally Educated Person" for a more
detailed discussion of these components.
    48. Emile Durkheim, "A Discussion on the Effective-
ness of Moral Doctrines," Bulletin de la Société Francaise
de Philosophie LX (May 20, 1907), pp. 219-231.
    49. Durkheim, Moral Education, p. 271.
    50. Ibid., p. 274. See also Durkheim, The Evolution
of Educational Thought, p. xxiv.
    51. Durkheim, Moral Education, pp. 252-257.
    52. Durkheim, "A Discussion on the Effectiveness of
Moral Doctrines," p. 129.
    53. Ibid., p. 130.
    54. Emile Durkheim, "A Discussion on Positive Moral-
ity: The Issue of Rationality in Ethics," in Durkheim:
Essays on Morals and Education, pp. 52-64.
    55. Ibid., pp. 59-60.
    56. Ibid., pp. 60-61.
    57. See, for example, Crittendon, Bearings in Moral
Education.
    58. Durkheim, "Contribution to 'Morality Without
God: An Attempt to Find a Collectivist Solution,'" La
Revue, LIX (1905), pp. 306-308; translated in Durkheim:
Essays on Morals and Education, p. 34.
    59. Durkheim, Moral Education, p. 21.
    60. Durkheim, "The Determination of Moral Facts,"
p. 35.
    61. Durkheim, Moral Education, p. 24.
    62. Ibid., p. 59.
    63. Ibid., pp. 23-115.
    64. Ibid., p. 50.
    65. Durkheim, "The Determination of Moral Facts,"
pp. 64-67.
    66. Durkheim, "Education: Its Nature and Role,"
p. 71.
    67. See, for example, Willis Moore, "Indoctrination
as a Normative Conception," Studies in Philosophy and
Education, IV, 4 (Summer 1966), pp. 396-403; also
Prakash, "Moral Education and the Initiation Into the
Institution of Morality."
    68. Durkheim, Moral Education, p. 271.
    69. Ibid., p. 266.
    70. Emile Durkheim, "The Role of the State in Educa-
tion," in Education and Sociology, p. 85.
    71. Durkheim, Moral Education, p. 18.

72. Durkheim, "The Role of the State in Education,"
p. 86.
73. Ibid., p. 89.
74. Durkheim, The Evolution of Educational Thought,
p. 24.
75. Ibid., p. 28.
76. Ibid., p. 30.
77. Ibid., chapter 1.
78. Ibid., p. 7.
79. Ibid., p. 8. See also chapter 14, "The Evolution
of the Role of Secondary Education in France," in Durkheim,
Education and Sociology.
80. This volume is regarded by Durkheim scholars as
one of Durkheim's important--and neglected--works: Lukes,
chapter 19 in Emile Durkheim, His Life and Work; Wallwork,
Durkheim: Morality and Milieu, p. 130.
81. Durkheim, Moral Education, p. 3.
82. Durkheim, "The Nature and Method of Pedagogy,"
in Education and Sociology, pp. 91-102.
83. Ibid., p. 101.
84. Ibid., p. 106.
85. Durkheim, Moral Education, p. 160. (See also
p. 150, where Durkheim speaks out against the use of
corporal punishment in schools.)
86. Emile Durkheim with F. Buisson, "Enfance," in
Nouveau dictionnaire de pédagogie et d'instruction
primaire (Paris: Hachette, 1911), pp. 552-553; translated
in Durkheim: Essays on Morals and Education, pp. 151-152.
87. Durkheim, Moral Education, pp. 228-235.
88. Ibid., p. 260.

CHAPTER 3. JOHN WILSON: MORAL
EDUCATION AS RATIONAL UTILITARIANISM

1. Wilson's deductive educational model represents
one prominent approach to the relationship between theory
and practice in education. See John Wilson, The Assessment of Morality (Windsor, Eng.: NFER-NELSON Publishing,
1973), p. vii; John Wilson, Practical Methods of Moral
Education (London: Heinemann Educational, 1972); John
Wilson, "Moral Education: Retrospect and Prospect," in
Journal of Moral Education, IX (October 1979), pp. 3-9.
2. John Wilson, Norman Williams, and Barry Sugarman,
Introduction to Moral Education (Harmondsworth, Eng.:
Penguin, 1967), p. 45.
3. Ibid., pp. 44-45.
4. John Harrison, "Review Article: John Wilson as
Moral Educator," Journal of Moral Education, VII, 1
(October 1977), p. 56.
5. John Wilson, Equality (London: Hutchinson, 1966),
p. 40; John Wilson, Education and the Concept of Mental
Health (London: Routledge and Kegan Paul, 1968), pp. 20-
22.
6. Wilson, Practical Methods of Moral Education,
pp. 92-116.

7. Harrison, "Review Article: John Wilson as Moral Educator," p. 56.

8. The Preface and General Introduction to <u>Introduction to Moral Education</u>, pp. 9-35, describe the realities which led Wilson to the development of a new approach.

9. Wilson, <u>The Assessment of Morality</u>, pp. 38-39, 43.

10. Ibid., p. 39.

11. Wilson, Williams, and Sugarman, <u>Introduction to Moral Education</u>, p. 26.

12. Wilson, <u>The Assessment of Morality</u>, pp. 60-67.

13. See the following for critical analyses of Wilson's work on this point in particular: Crittendon, <u>Bearings in Moral Education</u>, p. 37; Harrison, "Review Article: John Wilson as Moral Educator"; J. Martin Stafford, "John Wilson, Prophet of the Sane Society," <u>Journal of Philosophy of Education</u>, XXIII (1979), pp. 167-168; Mary Warnock, <u>Schools of Thought</u> (London: Faber and Faber, 1977), pp. 131-136.

14. Warnock, <u>Schools of Thought</u>, p. 132.

15. Stafford, "John Wilson, Prophet of the Sane Society," p. 169.

16. Ibid., p. 171.

17. Wilson, Williams, and Sugarman, <u>Introduction to Moral Education</u>, p. 192.

18. John Wilson, <u>Education in Religion and the Emotions</u> (London: Heinemann Educational, 1971), p. 45.

19. John Wilson, <u>Moral Thinking</u> (London: Heinemann Educational, 1970), p. 65.

20. Wilson, <u>The Assessment of Morality</u>, pp. 41, 50.

21. Stafford, "John Wilson: Prophet of the Sane Society," p. 175.

22. John Wilson, <u>Preface to the Philosophy of Education</u> (London: Routledge and Kegan Paul, 1979), p. 243. See footnote 24, where he directly responds to Warnock's criticism of his article, "Moral Education and the Curriculum," in <u>Progress and Problems in Moral Education</u>, Monica Taylor, ed. (Windsor, Eng.: NFER-NELSON Publishing, 1975), pp. 25-47; also Wilson's "Reply to J. Martin Stafford," <u>Journal of Philosophy of Education</u>, XXIII (1979), pp. 187-188.

23. Wilson, <u>The Assessment of Morality</u>, p. 42.

24. See the following discussion of this issue: W. Frankena, <u>Ethics</u>, 2d ed. (Englewood Cliffs, N.J.: Prentice-Hall, 1973).

25. For such a discussion, see G. J. Warnock, <u>The Object of Morality</u> (London: Methuen, 1971).

26. Wilson, Williams, and Sugarman, <u>Introduction to Moral Education</u>, pp. 95, 75, and 89; see also Wilson, chapter 3 in <u>Moral Thinking</u>.

27. Wilson, <u>Practical Methods of Moral Education</u>, pp. 20-30; Wilson, <u>Moral Thinking</u>, p. 17.

28. Stafford, "John Wilson: Prophet of the Sane Society," p. 171.

29. Warnock, <u>Schools of Thought</u>, p. 132.

30. This is a phrase that Wilson uses in an early essay as a criterion for distinguishing between 'education' and 'indoctrination'. See John Wilson, "Education and Indoctrination," in Aims in Education, T. H. B. Hollins, ed. (Manchester, Eng.: Manchester University Press, 1969), pp. 24–46.

31. Warnock, Schools of Thought, p. 131.

32. Wilson, The Assessment of Morality, p. 19. In this context he criticizes Kohlberg's theory for being too reductionist and for its unsatisfactory distinction between thought and action.

33. Wilson, Preface to the Philosophy of Education; John Wilson, Fantasy and Common Sense in Education (New York: John Wiley, 1979).

34. Wilson, The Assessment of Morality, pp. 38–39, represents a later formulation of the components. The major changes from earlier formulations are in (1) the breakdown of PHIL, EMP, and GIG into more detailed subcategories; (2) the consolidation of KRAT and the now defunct DIK.

35. Wilson, The Assessment of Morality, pp. 64–67.

36. For a critique of the deductive model in curriculum development, see Ian Westbury and Neil Wilcox, eds., Science, Curriculum, and Liberal Education: Selected Essays of Joseph J. Schwab (Chicago: University of Chicago Press, 1978).

37. Wilson, "Education and Indoctrination"; Wilson, Williams, and Sugarman, Introduction to Moral Education.

38. Wilson, "Education and Indoctrination," pp. 27–28.

39. R. M. Hare, "Adolescents into Adults," in Aims in Education, pp. 47–70.

40. Wilson, Williams, and Sugarman, Introduction to Moral Education, p. 171.

41. Wilson, Practical Methods of Moral Education, p. 14.

42. John Wilson, "Teaching and Neutrality," in Progress and Problems in Moral Education, Monica Taylor, ed. (Windsor, Eng.: NFER-NELSON Publishing, 1977), pp. 113–122; see also paper by Mary Warnock in the same volume, "The Neutral Teacher," pp. 103–112.

43. Taylor, ed., Progress and Problems in Moral Education, pp. 5–20.

44. Wilson, Williams, and Sugarman, Introduction to Moral Education, pp. 411–412.

45. Wilson, Practical Methods of Moral Education, pp. 111–149.

46. Ibid., p. 89.

CHAPTER 4. MORAL EDUCATION AS
VALUES CLARIFICATION

1. See Superka et al., eds., chapter 5 in Values Education Sourcebook; Howard Kirschenbaum and Sidney Simon, eds., "An Annotated Bibliography for Values

Clarification," Readings in Values Clarification (Minneapolis: Winston Press, 1973), pp. 363–383; Howard Kirschenbaum, "Values Clarification: An Annotated Bibliography, 1965–1975," appendix in Advanced Values Clarification (La Jolla, Calif.: University Associates, 1977), pp. 153–187.

2. Louis Raths, Merrill Harmin, and Sidney Simon, Values and Teaching: Working with Values in the Classroom (Columbus, Ohio: Charles E. Merrill, 1966); 2d ed., 1978.

3. Howard Kirschenbaum, "Beyond Values Clarification," in Readings in Values Clarification, pp. 92–110; Howard Kirschenbaum, "Clarifying Values Clarification: Some Theoretical Issues," in Moral Education: It Comes with the Territory, D. Purpel and K. Ryan, eds. (Berkeley, Calif.: McCutchan, 1976), pp. 116–125; Howard Kirschenbaum, Advanced Values Clarification.

4. Raths, Harmin, and Simon, Values and Teaching, 2d ed., pp. 16–23. See also C. Volkmor, A. Pasanella, L. Raths, Values in the Classroom (Columbus, Ohio: Charles E. Merrill, 1977), p. 1.

5. Raths, Harmin, and Simon, Values and Teaching, 2d ed., p. 34.

6. Volkmor, Pasanella, and Raths, Values in the Classroom, p. 47.

7. Milton Rokeach, "Towards a Philosophy of Values Education," in Values Education: Theory, Practice, Problems, Prospects, John Meyer, Brian Burnham, and John Cholvat, eds. (Waterloo, Ontario: Wilfrid Laurier University Press, 1975), p. 122. See also Milton Rokeach, "Values Education in Educational Settings," in Understanding Human Values: Individual and Societal, M. Rokeach, ed. (New York: Free Press, 1979), pp. 259–269.

8. Hugh Nevin, "Values Clarification: Perspectives on John Dewey with Implications for Religious Education," Religious Education, LXXXIV, 6 (November–December 1978), pp. 661–677.

9. John Stewart, "Problems and Contradictions of Values Clarification," Phi Delta Kappan, LVI, 10 (June 1975), pp. 684–689.

10. Kirschenbaum, "Clarifying Values Clarification: Some Theoretical Issues," p. 122.

11. VC_1: Raths, Harmin, and Simon, Values and Teaching, 2d ed., p. 28. VC_2: Kirschenbaum, "Clarifying Values Clarification"; (also modified) in Kirschenbaum, "Beyond Values Clarification," pp. 105–106.

12. Kirschenbaum, "Beyond Values Clarification," p. 100.

13. Ibid., p. 97.

14. A. C. Kazepides, "The Logic of Values Clarification," The Journal of Educational Thought, XI, 2 (August 1977), pp. 104, 110.

15. Raths, Harmin, and Simon, Values and Teaching, 2d ed., p. ix.

16. Sidney Simon and Sally Wendkos Olds, Helping Your Child Learn Right from Wrong: A Guide to Values Clarification (New York: Simon and Schuster, 1976), p. 17.

17. See, for example, Superka et al., eds., chapter

5 in Values Education Sourcebook; Richard Hersh, John
Miller, and Glen Fielding, "Valuing Process and Clarification Model," chapter 5 in Models of Moral Education
(New York: Longman, 1980); Purpel and Ryan, eds., "Part
II: The Values Clarification Approach," Moral Education:
It Comes with the Territory, pp. 69-170.
     18.   Kazepides, "The Logic of Values Clarification,"
p. 105.
     19.   Raths, Harmin, and Simon, Values and Teaching,
2d ed., pp. 329-337.
     20.   Raths, Harmin, and Simon, Values and Teaching,
p. 26.
     21.   Alan Lockwood, "A Critical View of Values Clari-
fication," Teachers College Record, LXXVII, 1 (September
1975), p. 93.
     22.   Kirschenbaum, "Beyond Values Clarification,"
p. 93.
     23.   Kazepides, "The Logic of Values Clarification,"
pp. 100-101.
     24.   Volkmor, Pasanella, and Raths, Values in the
Classroom, p. 1.
     25.   Simon and Olds, Helping Your Child Learn Right
from Wrong, p. 25.
     26.   Raths, Harmin, and Simon, Values and Teaching,
2d ed., p. 34.
     27.   Ibid.
     28.   Volkmor, Pasanella, and Raths, Values in the
Classroom, p. 22.
     29.   Kirschenbaum,"Clarifying Values Clarification:
Some Theoretical Issues," p. 122.
     30.   Raths, Harmin, and Simon, Values and Teaching,
2d ed., p. ix.
     31.   Stewart, "Problems and Contradictions of Values
Clarification," p. 150.
     32.   Rokeach, "Toward a Philosophy of Values Educa-
tion," p. 123.
     33.   Raths, Harmin, and Simon, Values and Teaching,
pp. 28-29.
     34.   Raths, Harmin, and Simon, "Values and Thinking,"
chapter 10 in Values and Teaching, 2d ed., pp. 200-226.
     35.   Kirschenbaum, "Clarifying Values Clarification:
Some Theoretical Issues," p. 124.
     36.   Kirschenbaum, Advanced Values Clarification,
p. 98.
     37.   A. C. Kazepides, "The Logic of Values Clarifi-
cation," pp. 100-101.
     38.   Simon and Olds, Helping Your Child Learn Right
from Wrong, p. 17.
     39.   Rokeach, "Towards a Philosophy of Values Educa-
tion," pp. 120-122.
     40.   Raths, Harmin, and Simon, Values and Teaching,
p. 30.
     41.   Kirschenbaum, "Clarifying Values Clarification:
Some Theoretical Issues," p. 121.
     42.   Raths, Harmin, and Simon, Values and Teaching,
pp. 59-66.

43. Simon and Olds, Helping Your Child Learn Right from Wrong, p. 29.
44. Kirschenbaum, "Beyond Values Clarification," p. 97.
45. Sidney Simon, "Values Clarification vs. Indoctrination," Social Education (December 1971), pp. 902-905.
46. Ibid., p. 902.
47. Howard Kirschenbaum and Sidney Simon, "Values and the Futures Movement in Education," in Readings in Values Clarification, p. 18.
48. Simon, "Values Clarification vs. Indoctrination," p. 127.
49. Simon and Olds, Helping Your Child Learn Right from Wrong, pp. 18-23.
50. Volkmor, Pasanella, and Raths, Values in the Classroom, p. 24.
51. Sidney Simon and Lawrence Kohlberg, "An Exchange of Opinion Between Kohlberg and Simon," Learning (December 1972), p. 62.
52. Sidney Simon, "A Reply to Stewart," Phi Delta Kappan, LVI, 10 (June 1975), p. 688.
53. Kirschenbaum, Advanced Values Clarification, p. 2.
54. Raths, Harmin, and Simon, Values and Teaching, 2d ed., pp. 55-56.
55. Ibid., p. 86.
56. Sidney Simon and P. O'Rourke, Developing Values with Exceptional Children (Englewood Cliffs, N.J.: Prentice-Hall, 1977).
57. Simon and Olds, Helping Your Child Learn Right from Wrong.
58. Gordon Hart, Values Clarification for Counselors (Springfield, Ill.: Charles C. Thomas, 1978).
59. Dov Peretz Elkins, Clarifying Jewish Values (Rochester, N.Y.: Growth Associates, 1977). Dov Peretz Elkins, Humanizing Jewish Life (South Brunswick, N.J.: A. S. Barnes, 1976).
60. Kirschenbaum, Advanced Values Clarification, p. 2.
61. Ibid., pp. 10-12.
62. Kirschenbaum, "Beyond Values Clarification," p. 97.
63. Kazepides, "The Logic of Values Clarification," p. 104.

CHAPTER 5. LAWRENCE KOHLBERG: THE COGNITIVE-DEVELOPMENTAL APPROACH TO MORAL EDUCATION

1. Edmund Sullivan, Kohlberg's Structuralism, Monograph Series 115 (Toronto: Ontario Institute for Studies in Education, 1977), p. 1.
2. Lawrence Kohlberg, "Moral Education in the Schools: A Developmental View," School Review, LXXIV, 1 (Spring 1966), p. 5. See also Lawrence Kohlberg with Rochelle Mayer, "Development as the Aim of Education: The Dewey View," in The Philosophy of Moral Development, Lawrence

Kohlberg, ed. (San Francisco: Harper & Row, 1981), pp. 55-59.

3.   A Bibliography of Kohlberg's writings may be found in Kohlberg, The Philosophy of Moral Development, pp. 423-428.

4.   Ibid.

5.   Sullivan, Kohlberg's Structuralism, p. 15.

6.   Kohlberg, The Philosophy of Moral Development, p. xvii. See also "Symposium on Moral Development," Ethics, XCI, 3 (April 1982), p. 407.

7.   Kohlberg, The Philosophy of Moral Development, p. 4.

8.   Herbert Saltzstein, "Critical Issues in Kohlberg's Theory of Moral Reasoning," in Monographs of the Society for Research in Child Development, XLVIII, 1-2 (1983).

9.   Kohlberg with Mayer, "Development as the Aim of Education: The Dewey View," pp. 51-54.

10.   Ibid., p. 59.

11.   Lawrence Kohlberg, "Revisions in the Theory and Practice of Moral Development," in New Directions for Child Development: Moral Education, No. 2, William Damon, ed. (San Francisco: Jossey-Bass, 1978), p. 85.

12.   Lawrence Kohlberg, "Educating for a Just Society: An Updated and Revised Statement," in Moral Development, Moral Education, and Kohlberg, Brenda Munsey, ed. (Birmingham, Ala.: Religious Education Press, 1980), pp. 455-470. Lawrence Kohlberg, "High School Democracy and Educating for a Just Society," in Moral Education: A First Generation of Research and Development, Ralph Mosher, ed. (New York: Praeger, 1980), pp. 20-57.

13.   William Sullivan, Reconstructing Public Philosophy (Berkeley, Calif.: University of California Press, 1983).

14.   Lawrence Kohlberg, "Moral Development, Religious Thinking, and the Question of a Seventh Stage," in The Philosophy of Moral Development, p. 318.

15.   Ibid., p. 319.

16.   Lawrence Kohlberg, "The Child as Moral Philosopher," Psychology Today (September 1968), p. 30.

17.   Sullivan, Kohlberg's Structuralism, p. 8.

18.   See Frankena's discussion of Sidgwick's attempt to synthesize deontologism and utilitarianism: William Frankena, "Lecture One: What Is Morality?" in Thinking About Morality (Ann Arbor: University of Michigan Press, 1980), p. 16.

19.   Lawrence Kohlberg, "From Is to Ought: How to Commit the Naturalistic Fallacy and Get Away With It in the Study of Moral Development," in The Philosophy of Moral Development, pp. 173-174.

20.   Lawrence Kohlberg, "Justice as Reversibility: The Claim to Moral Adequacy of a Highest Stage of Moral Development," in The Philosophy of Moral Development, p. 220.

21.   Ibid.

22.   Kohlberg with Mayer, "Development as the Aim of

Education: The Dewey View," p. 68.

23. Kohlberg, "From Is to Ought," pp. 170-172.

24. Lawrence Kohlberg, "Education for Justice: A Modern Statement of the Socratic View," in The Philosophy of Moral Development, p. 39.

25. Kohlberg, "From Is to Ought," p. 144.

26. Lawrence Kohlberg, "Why a Higher Stage Is a Better Stage," in Collected Papers on Moral Development and Moral Education, Lawrence Kohlberg, ed. (Cambridge, Mass.: Harvard Graduate School of Education, 1975), pp. 11-12.

27. Kohlberg, table 1, in "From Is to Ought," p. 165.

28. Dwight Boyd, "The Rawls Connection," in Moral Development, Moral Education, and Kohlberg, pp. 186, 191.

29. Kohlberg, "From Is to Ought," pp. 177-178.

30. Barry Bull, "Kohlberg's Place in a Theory of the Legitimate Role of Value in Public Education," in Philosophy of Education, 1978, Garry Fenstermacher, ed. (Champaign, Ill.: Philosophy of Education Society, 1979), p. 71.

31. R. S. Peters, "Moral Development: A Plea for Pluralism" and "The Place of Kohlberg's Theory in Moral Education," in Moral Development and Moral Education, R. S. Peters, ed. (London: George Allen and Unwin, 1981), pp. 92-103 and pp. 171-177.

32. One of the most comprehensive discussions of major theories of morality is to be found in John Dewey, Theory of the Moral Life (New York: Holt, Rinehart and Winston, 1960).

33. Kohlberg, "Moral Development, Religious Thinking, and the Question of a Seventh Stage," p. 321.

34. R. M. Hare, The Language of Morals (New York: Oxford University Press, 1964); R. M. Hare, Freedom and Reason (New York: Oxford University Press, 1965).

35. Brenda Munsey Mapel, "An Act-Theory Alternative to Rationalistic Moral Education," in Philosophy of Education, 1978, pp. 85-104; Clive Beck, "Rationalism in Kohlberg's Morality and Moral Education," in Philosophy of Education, 1978, pp. 105-111.

36. Peters, "The Place of Kohlberg's Theory in Moral Education." See also William Alston, "Comments on Kohlberg's 'From Is to Ought,'" in Cognitive Development and Epistemology, Theodore Mischel, ed. (New York: Academic Press, 1971), pp. 178-282.

37. Kohlberg, "From Is to Ought," p. 170.

38. Lawrence Kohlberg, "Stages of Moral Development as a Basis for Moral Education," in Moral Education: Interdisciplinary Approaches, C. M. Beck, B. S. Crittendon, E. V. Sullivan, eds. (Toronto: University of Toronto Press, 1971), p. 57.

39. Kohlberg, "Educating for a Just Society: An Updated and Revised Statement," p. 466.

40. Alston, "Comments on Kohlberg's 'From Is to Ought,'" p. 277.

41. Kohlberg, "Stages of Moral Development as a

Basis for Moral Education," p. 60.

42. H. Rorvik, "Content and Form in Kohlberg's Theory of Moral Development," Scandinavian Journal of Educational Research, XXIV, 3 (1980), p. 108.

43. Lawrence Kohlberg and Elliot Turiel, "Moral Development and Moral Education," in Psychology and Educational Practice, Gerald Lesser, ed. (Glenview, Ill.: Scott, Foresman, 1971), p. 414.

44. Peters, "Moral Development: A Plea for Pluralism," pp. 95-104. See also R. S. Peters, "Reason and Habit: the Paradox of Moral Education," in Moral Education in a Changing Society, W. R. Niblett, ed. (London: Faber and Faber, 1963); "The Cognitive and the Affective in Moral Action" [Discussion], in Moral Education: Interdisciplinary Approaches, pp. 373-402.

45. Augusto Blasi, "Bridging Moral Cognition and Moral Action: A Critical Review of the Literature," Psychological Bulletin, LXXXVIII, 1 (July 1980), p. 2.

46. See collections of Kohlberg's essays edited by Munsey, by Mosher, and in the journal Ethics; also Kohlberg's essay with Daniel Candee, "The Relations Between Moral Judgment and Moral Action," in The Psychology of Moral Development, Lawrence Kohlberg, ed. (San Francisco: Harper & Row, 1983). See also the articles by Kohlberg, Colby, Powers, and Reimer in New Directions for Child Development: Moral Education.

47. Kohlberg, "From Is to Ought," pp. 183-186.

48. Clark Power and Joseph Reimer, "Moral Atmosphere: An Educational Bridge Between Moral Judgment and Action," in New Directions for Child Development: Moral Education, pp. 105-116.

49. Ibid., p. 106.

50. See the following for a detailed report of the twenty-year, longitudinal study of moral development: Anne Colby, Lawrence Kohlberg, John Gibbs, and Marcus Lieberman, "A Longitudinal Study of Moral Judgment," in Monographs of the Society for Research on Child Development, XLVIII, 1-2 (1983).

51. Lawrence Kohlberg, "Indoctrination Versus Relativity," in The Philosophy of Moral Development, p. 7.

52. Kohlberg, The Philosophy of Moral Development, pp. 74-76.

53. Lawrence Kohlberg, "Revisions in the Theory and Practice of Moral Development," in New Directions for Child Development: Moral Education, p. 84.

54. Ibid.

55. Kohlberg and Turiel, "Moral Development and Moral Education," pp. 450-454. See also the following for a helpful discussion of the teacher in Kohlberg's theory: Richard Hersh, Diane Pritchard Paolitto, Joseph Reimar, Promoting Moral Growth (New York: Longman, 1979), pp. 133-201.

56. Kohlberg, "Revisions in the Theory and Practice of Moral Development," p. 84.

57. Practical strategies and dilemmas are described

in several sets of teacher guides. See, for example:
Thomas Lickona et al., A Strategy for Teaching Values
(New York: Guidance Associates, 1972)--includes discussion guide, filmstrips, and cassettes; Nancy Porter and
Nancy Taylor, How To Assess the Moral Reasoning of Students (Toronto: Ontario Institute for Studies in Education, 1972).
    58.   Elsa Wasserman, "An Alternative High School Based
on Kohlberg's Just Community Approach to Moral Education,"
in Moral Education: A First Generation of Research and
Development, pp. 265-278.
    59.   Lawrence Kohlberg, "Cognitive-Developmental
Theory and the Practice of Collectivist Moral Education,"
in Group Care: An Israeli Approach: the Educational Path
of Youth Aliyah, Martin Wolins and Meir Gottesman, eds.
(New York: Gordon and Breach, 1971), pp. 355-358.
    60.   Lawrence Kohlberg, "Education for Justice: The
Vocation of Janusz Korczak," in The Philosophy of Moral
Development, p. 402.
    61.   Moshe Blatt and Lawrence Kohlberg, "The Effects
of Classroom Moral Discussion upon Children's Level of
Moral Judgment," Journal of Moral Education, IV, 2 (1975),
p. 137.
    62.   Materials produced up to 1976 are systematically
listed and analyzed in Superka et al., Values Education
Sourcebook, pp. 31-53.
    63.   Linda Rosenzweig, "Kohlberg in the Classroom,"
in Moral Development, Moral Education, and Kohlberg,
pp. 359-380.
    64.   Kohlberg, "Revisions in the Theory and Practice
of Moral Development," p. 85.
    65.   Kohlberg, "Educating for a Just Society," p. 457.
    66.   Ibid.

CHAPTER 6.
AGAINST MORAL EDUCATION

    1.   What I have loosely called 'the anti-moral educa-
tion tradition' encompasses a huge span of time and writings; a select list of examples of this tradition appears
in the bibliography. The following present overviews of
aspects of the tradition: Paul Avrich, The Modern School
Movement: Anarchism and Education in the United States
(Princeton: Princeton University Press, 1980); Diane
Ravitch, The Revisionists Revised: A Critique of the Radi-
cal Attack on the Schools (New York: Basic Books, 1978);
Brian Simon, ed., The Radical Tradition in Education in
Britain (London: Lawrence and Wishart, 1972); Joel Spring,
A Primer of Libertarian Education (Montreal: Black Rose
Books, 1975).
    2.   George Dennison, The Lives of Children (New York:
Random House, 1969); Ivan Illich, De-Schooling Society
(New York: Harper & Row, 1971); Herbert Kohl, 36 Children

(London: Victor Gollancz, 1968); Jonathan Kozol, Death at an Early Age (New York: Bantam Books, 1967); George Leonard, Education and Ecstasy (New York: Delta Books, 1968); Neil Postman and Charles Weingartner, Teaching as a Subversive Activity (New York: Delacorte, 1969); David Nyberg, ed., The Philosophy of Open Education (London: Routledge and Kegan Paul, 1971).

3. Samuel Bowles and Herbert Gintis, Schooling in Capitalist America: Educational Reform and the Contradiction of Economic Life (New York: Basic Books, 1976); Walter Feinberg, Reason and Rhetoric: The Intellectual Foundations of 20th Century Liberal Educational Policy (New York: John Wiley, 1975); Michael Katz, Class, Bureaucracy and Schools (New York: Praeger, 1971); Michael Katz, The Irony of Early School Reform (Boston: Beacon Press, 1968); Ravitch, The Revisionists Revised: A Critique of the Radical Attack on the Schools; Joel Spring, American Education: An Introduction to Social and Political Aspects (New York: Longman, 1978); Joel Spring, Education and the Rise of the Corporate State (Boston: Beacon Press, 1972).

4. Joel Spring, Education and the Rise of the Corporate State.

5. Bowles and Gintis, Schooling in Capitalist America.

6. Francisco Ferrer, The Origins and Ideas of the Modern School (reprint, New York: Arno Press, 1972).

7. Lev Tolstoi, Tolstoy on Education (Chicago: University of Chicago Press, 1967); Charles Badouin, Tolstoi: The Teacher (London: Kegan Paul, Trench Trubner, 1923).

8. Katz, Class, Bureaucracy and Schools, p. 117.

9. Illich, De-Schooling Society, pp. 1-24; Leonard, Education and Ecstasy, pp. 16-21.

10. Avrich, The Modern School Movement, p. 47.

11. There have been several analyses of individual thinkers associated with the 'tradition', e.g., Tolstoy, Neil, Stirner, Ferrer, Goldman, Bakunin, and Godwin; however, there has not been an extensive literature that has dealt with general motifs of the tradition.

12. John Wilson, "Education and Indoctrination," in Aims in Education, T. H. B. Hollins, ed. (Manchester, Eng.: Manchester University Press, 1969), pp. 24-46.

13. Ferrer, The Origins and Ideals of the Modern School, pp. 15-17, 19-22.

14. Bruce Calvert, Rational Education (Griffith, Ind.: Open Road Press, 1911), p. 25.

15. Carl Bereiter, Must We Educate? (Englewood Cliffs, N.J.: Prentice-Hall, 1973).

16. Ibid., pp. 13-15.

17. Ibid., pp. 36-37.

18. Ibid., p. 37.

19. According to Spring, the phrase was coined by Max Stirner. See Spring, A Primer of Libertarian Education, p. 37; Max Stirner, The Ego and His Own (New York: Libertarian Book Club, 1963); Max Stirner, The False Principle of Our Education (Colorado Springs, Colo.:

Ralph Myles, 1967). See also: R. W. K. Paterson, The
Nihilist Egoist: Max Stirner (London: Oxford University
Press, 1971); John Carroll, Breakout from the Crystal
Palace: The Anarcho-Psychological Critique: Stirner,
Nietzsche, Dostoevsky (London: Routledge and Kegan Paul,
1974).

20. See the following discussion of the "gardener"
and the "sculptor" models of education: Martin Buber,
"On National Education," in Israel and the World, Martin
Buber, ed. (New York: Schocken, 1963), pp. 148-149.

21. Spring, A Primer of Libertarian Education, p. 10.

22. A. S. Neil, The Problem Child (New York: Robert
McBride, 1927), p. 17.

23. Ferrer, The Origins and Ideas of the Modern
School, p. 45; Michael Bakunin, God and the State (New
York: Dover Publications, 1970), pp. 36-38; G. P. Maximoff,
"Upbringing and Education," chapter 12 in The Political
Philosophy of Bakunin (New York: Free Press, 1953),
pp. 327-337.

24. Illich, De-Schooling Society, p. 34.

25. Bowles and Gintis, "Beyond the Educational Fron-
tier: The Great American Dream Freeze" and "Education,
Socialism, and the Revolution," chapter 1 and chapter 11
in Schooling in Capitalist America.

26. Shulamith Firestone, "Down with Childhood,"
chapter 4 in The Dialectic of Sex (Houston: Paladin,
1970). See also: Jane Roland Martin, "Sophie and Emile:
A Case Study of Sex Bias in the History of Educational
Thought," Harvard Educational Review, LI, 3 (August 1981),
pp. 357-373; Jane Roland Martin, "Excluding Women from the
Educational Realm," Harvard Educational Review, LII, 2
(May 1983), pp. 133-148; Jane Roland Martin, "The Ideal
of the Educated Person," Educational Theory, XXXI, 2
(Spring 1981), pp. 97-109.

27. Bowles and Gintis, Schooling in Capitalist
America, p. 11; Feinberg, chapters 2 and 3 in Reason
and Rhetoric; Katz, Class, Bureaucracy and Schools,
p. 118: "Most starkly, both Addams and Dewey in the last
analysis stressed the subservience of individual will and
operation to those of the group."

28. Bowles and Gintis, chapters 1-7 in Schooling in
Capitalist America.

29. Bowles and Gintis, "Broken Promises: School Reform in Retrospect," chapter 2 in Schooling in Capitalist
America.

30. Bowles and Gintis, Schooling in Capitalist
America, p. 199.

31. Ibid., p. 252.

32. Lawrence Kohlberg, "Moral Development in the
Schools: A Developmental View," The School Review, LXXIV,
1 (Spring 1966), pp. 3-6.

33. Alice Miel, The Short-Changed Children of
Suburbia (New York: Institute of Human Relations Press,
1967).

34. Katz, Class, Bureaucracy and Schools, p. xviii.

35. Feinberg, Reason and Rhetoric, p. vi.
36. Robert Dreeben, chapter 5 in On What Is Learned
in School (Reading, Mass.: Addison-Wesley, 1968), pp. 63-
90.
37. Talcott Parsons, "The School as a Social System:
Some of Its Functions in American Society," Harvard Educational Review, XXIX, 4 (1959), pp. 297-318.

CHAPTER 7. DEWEY AND HIS FRIENDS
TALK TOGETHER

1. See the following comprehensive bibliography of
writings by and on Dewey: Jo Ann Boydston, ed., Guide to
the Works of John Dewey (Carbondale and Edwardsville,
Ill.: Southern Illinois University Press, 1970); Jo Ann
Boydston and Kathleen Poulos, eds., Checklist of Writings
About John Dewey, 2d ed. (Carbondale, Ill.: Southern
Illinois University Press, 1974).
The following are useful resources for the discussions
of Dewey and moral education: William Frankena, chapter 4
in Three Historical Philosophies of Education (Glenview,
Ill.: Scott, Foresman, 1965); James Gouinlock, John Dewey's
Philosophy of Value (New York: Humanities Press, 1972);
James Gouinlock, ed., The Moral Writings of John Dewey
(New York: Hafner Press, 1971); Sidney Hook, "Part I:
Studies in the Educational Philosophy of John Dewey," in
Education and the Taming of Power (London: Alcove Press,
1974), pp. 1-202; Joseph Ratner, ed., Intelligence in the
Modern World: John Dewey's Philosophy (New York: Modern
Library, 1939); Israel Scheffler, part 4 in Four Pragma-
tists (London: Routledge and Kegan Paul, 1974).
2. This topic is developed in detail by Dewey in
Human Nature and Conduct (New York: Modern Library, 1922).
See also an address delivered before the College of Physi-
cians in St. Louis, April 21, 1937, and published in
Intelligence in the Modern World: John Dewey's Philosophy,
pp. 817-834. See also John Dewey, "Man, Nature, and
Society," chapter 3 in The Moral Writings of John Dewey,
J. Gouinlock, ed., pp. 23-55.
3. John Dewey, Theory of the Moral Life (New York:
Holt, Rinehart and Winston, 1960), p. 80.
4. Emile Durkheim, The Division of Labor in Society
(New York: Macmillan, 1933), p. 398.
5. Lawrence Kohlberg with Rochelle Mayer, "Development as the Aim of Education: The Dewey View," in The
Philosophy of Moral Development, p. 55.
6. John Dewey, Moral Principles in Education (Carbondale, Ill.: Arcturus Books, Southern Illinois University
Press, 1975), p. 7.
7. Ibid., p. 11.
8. Wilson, The Assessment of Morality, p. 38.
9. Dewey, "Moral Judgment and Knowledge," chapter 5
in Theory of the Moral Life, pp. 120-146; Dewey, "The
Nature of Principles," in Human Nature and Conduct,
pp. 238-247.

10. Dewey, "The Nature and Office of Principles," in Theory of the Moral Life, pp. 136-145.

11. John Dewey, Problems of Men (New York: Philosophical Library, 1946).

12. Scheffler, Four Pragmatists, p. 195.

13. Dewey, Theory of the Moral Life, p. 134.

14. John Dewey, "The Place of Intelligence in Conduct," in Human Nature and Conduct, pp. 172-277; John Dewey, Logic: The Theory of Inquiry (New York: Holt, Rinehart and Winston, 1938), pp. 95-180; John Dewey, "Value and Intelligence," in The Moral Writings of John Dewey, J. Gouinlock, ed., pp. 122-157.

15. Dewey, Theory of the Moral Life, pp. 128-132; John Dewey, "Desire and Intelligence," in Human Nature and Conduct, pp. 48-264.

16. John Dewey, "The Place of Habit in Conduct," in Human Nature and Conduct, pp. 13-88.

17. Mary Warnock, Ethics Since 1900 (London: Oxford University Press, 1960).

18. John Dewey, Theory of Valuation (Chicago: International Encyclopedia of Unified Science, University of Chicago, 1939); Dewey, Theory of the Moral Life, pp. 128-130.

19. Dewey, chapter 5 in Theory of the Moral Life; John Dewey, "The Psychological Aspects of Moral Education," chapter 5 in Moral Principles in Education, pp. 45-58.

20. Dewey uses the word 'religious' to characterize such a holistic world view or attitude. John Dewey, A Common Faith (New Haven: Yale University Press, 1934), pp. 1-28.

21. R. S. Peters, "General Editor's Note," in Educational Judgment, James F. Doyle, ed. (London: Routledge and Kegan Paul, International Library of the Philosophy of Education, 1973), p. vii.

22. Willis Moore, "Indoctrination as a Normative Conception," Studies in Philosophy and Education, IV, 4 (Summer 1966); reprinted in Concepts of Indoctrination. I. A. Snook, ed. (London: Routledge and Kegan Paul, 1972), p. 95.

23. I. A. Snook, Indoctrination and Education (London: Routledge and Kegan Paul, 1972); I. A. Snook, ed., Concepts of Indoctrination.

24. Moore, "Indoctrination as a Normative Conception," p. 93.

25. John Dewey and Goodwin Watson, "The Forward View: A Free Teacher in a Free Society," in The Teacher and Society, W. Kilpatrick, ed. (New York: Appleton-Century, 1937), p. 332.

26. John Dewey, The Child and the Curriculum/The School and Society (Chicago: Phoenix Books, the University of Chicago Press, 1963), p. 23.

BIBLIOGRAPHY

Alston, William. "Comments on Kohlberg's 'From Is to Ought.'" In Cognitive Development and Epistemology, T. Mischel, ed. New York: Academic Press, 1971.

Archambault, Reginald, ed. Dewey on Education. New York: Random House, 1966.

Aron, Israelita Ettenberg, "Moral Education: The Formalist Tradition and the Deweyian Alternative." In Moral Development, Moral Education, and Kohlberg, Brenda Munsey, ed. Birmingham, Ala.: Religious Education Press, 1980.

Arvid, Adell. "Values Clarification Revised." The Christian Century, XCIII, 16 (May 5, 1976), p. 436.

Avrich, Paul. The Modern School Movement: Anarchism and Education in the United States. Princeton: Princeton University Press, 1980.

Badouin, Charles. Tolstoi: The Teacher. London: Kegan Paul, Trench Trubner, 1923.

Bakunin, Michael. God and the State. New York: Dover Publications, 1970.

Barrow, Robin. Moral Philosophy for Education. London: George Allen and Unwin, 1975.

Beck, Clive. "Rationalism in Kohlberg's Morality and Moral Education." In Philosophy of Education, 1978, Gary Fenstermacher, ed., pp. 105-111. Champaign, Ill.: Philosophy of Education Society, 1979.

Beck, Clive, Brian Crittendon, and Edmund Sullivan, eds. Moral Education: Interdisciplinary Approaches. Toronto: University of Toronto Press, 1971.

Bellah, Robert. Emile Durkheim on Morality and Society. Chicago: University of Chicago Press, 1973.

Bereiter, Carl. Must We Educate? Englewood Cliffs, N.J.: Prentice-Hall, 1973.

Beversluis, Eric. "The Dilemma of Values Clarification." In Philosophy of Education, 1978, Gary Fenstermacher, ed., pp. 417-427. Champaign, Ill.: Philosophy of Education Society, 1979.

Blasi, Augusto. "Bridging Moral Cognition and Moral Action: A Critical Review of the Literature." Psychological Bulletin, LXXXVIII, 1 (July 1980), pp. 1-45.

Blatt, Moshe, and Lawrence Kohlberg. "The Effects of Classroom Moral Discussion upon Children's Level of Moral Judgment." Journal of Moral Education, IV, 2 (1975), pp. 129-161.

Bowles, Samuel, and Herbert Gintis. Schooling in Capi-
    talist America: Educational Reform and the Contradic-
    tions of Economic Life. New York: Basic Books, 1976.
Boydston, Jo Ann, ed. Guide to the Works of John Dewey.
    Carbondale and Edwardsville, Ill.: Southern Illinois
    University Press, 1970.
Boydston, Jo Ann, and Kathleen Poulos, eds. Checklist
    of Writings About John Dewey, 2d ed. Carbondale, Ill.:
    Southern Illinois University Press, 1974.
Broudy, Harry, Michael J. Parsons, Ivan A. Snook, and
    Ronald D. Szoke. Philosophy of Education: An Organi-
    zation of Topics and Selected Sources. Urbana: Uni-
    versity of Illinois Press, 1967.
Buber, Martin. "On National Education." In Israel and
    the World, Martin Buber, ed. New York: Schocken,
    1963, pp. 149-166.
Bull, Barry. "Kohlberg's Place in a Theory of the Legiti-
    mate Role of Value in Public Education." In Philo-
    sophy of Education, 1978, Gary Fenstermacher, ed.,
    pp. 70-84. Champaign, Ill.: Philosophy of Education
    Society, 1979.
Calvert, Bruce. Rational Education. Griffith, Ind.:
    Open Road Press, 1911.
Carroll, John. Breakout from the Crystal Palace: The
    Anarcho-Psychological Critique: Stirner, Neitzsche,
    Dostoevsky. London: Routledge and Kegan Paul, 1974.
Casteel, J. Doyle, and Robert Stahl. Value Clarification
    in the Classroom: A Primer. Pacific Palisades, Calif.;
    Goodyear, 1975.
Chazan, Barry. "Holy Community and Values Education." In
    Moral Development Foundations: Theological Alterna-
    tives, Donald Joy, ed. Nashville: Abington Press,
    1982.
_____. "Kohlberg and Jewish Education." In Kohlberg and
    Moral Education: The Debate in Philosophy, Psychology,
    Religion and Education, Brenda Munsey, ed. Birming-
    ham, Ala.: Religious Education Press, 1980.
_____. The Language of Jewish Education. Bridgeport,
    Conn.: Hartmore House, 1978.
Chazan, Barry, and Jonas Soltis, eds. Moral Education.
    New York: Teachers College Press, 1973.
Cochrane, P. B., C. M. Hamm, and A. C. Kazepides, eds.
    The Domain of Moral Education. New York and Toronto:
    Paulist Press and Ontario Institute for Studies in
    Education, 1979.
Colby, Anne. "Evolution of a Moral-Developmental Theory."
    In New Directions for Child Development: Moral Edu-
    cation, No. 2, William Damon, ed., pp. 89-104. San
    Francisco: Jossey-Bass, 1978.
Colby, Anne, Lawrence Kohlberg, John Gibbs, and Marcus
    Lieberman. "A Longitudinal Study of Moral Judgment."
    Monographs of the Society for Research in Child
    Development, XLVIII, 1-2 (1983), pp. 1-96.
Colby, Anne, Lawrence Kohlberg, Edwin Fenton, Betsy
    Speicher-Dubin, and Marcus Lieberman. "Secondary

School Moral Discussion Programs Led by Social Studies
Teachers." Journal of Moral Education, VI, 2 (January
1977), pp. 90-111.

Crittendon, Brian. Bearings in Moral Education. Hawthorn,
Victoria, Australia: Australian Council for Educational
Research, 1978.

_____. "Durkheim: Sociology of Knowledge and Educational
Theory." Studies in Philosophy and Education, IV, 2
(Fall 1965), pp. 207-254.

Damon, William, ed. New Directions for Child Development:
Moral Education, No. 2. San Francisco, Jossey-Bass,
1978.

Davy, G. "Durkheim: II--l'oeuvre." Revue de Métaphysique
et de Morale, XXVII, pp. 71-112.

Dennison, George. The Lives of Children. New York: Random House, 1969.

Dewey, John. The Child and the Curriculum/The School and
Society. Chicago: Phoenix Books, University of Chicgo
Press, 1963.

_____. A Common Faith. New Haven: Yale University Press,
1934.

_____. Democracy and Education. New York: Macmillan,
1961.

_____. The Early Works, 1882-1898. Vols. 1-5. Carbondale
and Edwardsville, Ill.: Southern Illinois University
Press, Feffer and Simons, 1969.

_____. Experience and Education. New York: Collier Books,
1963.

_____. Experience and Nature. New York: W. W. Norton,
1929.

_____. Human Nature and Conduct. New York: Modern
Library, 1922.

_____. Logic: The Theory of Inquiry. New York: Holt,
Rinehart and Winston, 1938.

_____. Moral Principles in Education. Carbondale, Ill.:
Arcturus Books, Southern Illinois University Press,
1975.

_____. Problems of Men. New York: Philosophical Library,
1946.

_____. Theory of the Moral Life. New York: Holt, Rine-
hart and Winston, 1960.

_____. Theory of Valuation. Chicago: International Ency-
clopedia of Unified Science, University of Chicago,
1939.

Dewey, John, with James Hayden Tufts. Ethics. New York:
Henry Holt, 1908.

Dewey, John, and Goodwin Watson. "The Forward View: A
Free Teacher in a Free Society." In The Teacher and
Society, William Kilpatrick, ed., pp. 330-346. New
York: Appleton-Century, 1937.

Dreeben, Robert. On What Is Learned in School. Reading,
Mass.: Addison-Wesley, 1968.

Durkheim, Emile. "A Discussion on the Effectiveness of
Moral Doctrines." Bulletin de la Société Francaise
de Philosophie, LX (May 20, 1907), pp. 219-231.

Durkheim, Emile. The Division of Labor in Society. New
    York: Macmillan, 1933.
_____. Education and Philosophy. Glencoe, Ill.: Free
    Press, 1953.
_____. Education and Sociology. New York: Free Press,
    1956.
_____. Essays on Morals and Education, W. S. F. Pickering,
    ed. London: Routledge and Kegan Paul, 1979.
_____. The Evolution of Educational Thought. London:
    Routledge and Kegan Paul, 1977.
_____. Moral Education. New York: Free Press, 1961.
_____. Professional Ethics and Civic Morals. Glencoe,
    Ill.: Free Press, 1958.
_____. The Rules of Sociological Method. Glencoe, Ill.:
    Free Press, 1950.
_____. Sociology and Philosophy. Glencoe, Ill.: Free
    Press, 1953.
_____. Suicide: A Study in Sociology. Glencoe, Ill.:
    Free Press, 1952.
Durkheim, Emile, with F. Buisson. "Enfance" ("Childhood").
    In Nouveau dictionnaire de pédagogie et d'instruction
    primaire, pp. 552-553. Paris: Hachette, 1911.
Elkins, Dov Peretz. Clarifying Jewish Values. Rochester,
    N.Y.: Growth Associates, 1977.
_____. Humanizing Jewish Life. South Brunswick, N.J.:
    A. S. Barnes, 1976.
Feinberg, Walter. Reason and Rhetoric: The Intellectual
    Foundations cf 20th Century Liberal Educational
    Policy. New York: John Wiley, 1975.
Ferrer, Francisco. The Origins and Ideas of the Modern
    School. Reprint. New York: Arno Press, 1972.
Firestone, Shulamith. The Dialectic of Sex. Houston,
    Paladin, 1970.
Flanagan, Owen J. "Virtue, Sex and Gender: Some Philo-
    sophic Reflections on the Moral Psychology Debate."
    Ethics, XCII, 3 (April 1982), pp. 499-512.
Fowler, James W. Stages of Faith. New York: Harper &
    Row, 1981.
Fraenkel, Jack. How to Teach About Values: An Analytic
    Approach. Englewood Cliffs, N.J.: Prentice-Hall,
    1977.
Frankena, William. Ethics. 2d ed. Englewood Cliffs,
    N.J.: Prentice-Hall, 1973.
_____. Thinking About Morality. Ann Arbor: The Univer-
    sity of Michigan Press, 1980.
_____. Three Historical Philosophies of Education. Glen-
    view, Ill.: Scott, Foresman, 1965.
Freud, Sigmund. Civilization and Its Discontents. New
    York: W. W. Norton, 1961.
Gilligan, Carol. In a Different Voice: Psychological
    Theory and Women's Development. Cambridge, Mass.:
    Harvard University Press, 1982.
Goldstein, Marc. "Durkheim's Sociology of Education:
    Interpretations of Social Change Through Education."
    Educational Theory, XXVI, 3 (Summer 1970), pp. 289-297.

Goodpaster, Kenneth. "Kohlbergian Theory: A Philosophical
    Counter-Invitation," Ethics, XCII, 3 (April 1982),
    pp. 491-498.
Gouinlock, James. John Dewey's Philosophy of Value. New
    York: Humanities Press, 1972.
____, ed. The Moral Writings of John Dewey. New York:
    Hafner Press, 1971.
Greer, Colin. Cobweb Attitudes: Essays on Educational and
    Cultural Mythology. New York: Teachers College Press,
    1970.
____. The Great School Legend. New York: Basic Books,
    1972.
Hall, Robert. Moral Education: A Handbook for Teachers.
    Minneapolis: Winston Press, 1979.
Hare, R. M. Freedom and Reason. New York: Oxford Uni-
    versity Press, 1965.
____. The Language of Morals. New York: Oxford Univer-
    sity Press, 1964.
Harmin, Merrill. What I've Learned About Values Educa-
    tion. Bloomington, Ind.: Phi Delta Kappa Educational
    Foundation, 1977.
Harmin, Merrill, Howard Kirschenbaum, and Sidney Simon.
    Clarifying Values Through Subject Matter. Minnea-
    polis: Winston Press, 1973.
Harrison, John. "Review Article: John Wilson as Moral
    Educator." Journal of Moral Education, VII, 1
    (October 1977), pp. 50-63.
____. "Values Clarification: An Appraisal." Journal of
    Moral Education, VI, 1 (October 1976), pp. 22-31.
Hart, Gordon. Values Clarification for Counselors.
    Springfield, Ill.: Charles C. Thomas, 1978.
Hawley, Robert. Human Values in the Classroom. Amherst,
    Mass.: Education Research Associates, 1973.
Henriot, J. Existence et obligation. Paris: P. U. F.,
    1967.
Hersh, Richard, John Miller, and Glen Fielding. Models
    of Moral Education. New York: Longman, 1980.
Hersh, Richard, and Diane Paolitto. "The Teacher as
    Moral Educator." In Value/Moral Education: Schools
    and Teachers, Thomas Hennessy, ed. New York: Paulist
    Press, 1979.
Hersh, Richard, Diane Pritchard Paolitto, and Joseph
    Reimar. Promoting Moral Growth. New York: Longman,
    1979.
Hirst, P. Q. Durkheim, Bernard, and Epistemology.
    London: Routledge and Kegan Paul, 1975.
Hoffmann, M. L. "Development of Moral Thought, Feeling,
    and Behavior." American Psychologist, XXXIV, 10
    (October 1979), pp. 958-966.
Hollins, T. H. B., ed. Aims in Education. Manchester,
    Eng.: Manchester University Press, 1969.
Holmes, Mark. "Moral Education: What Can Schools Do?"
    Interchange, VII, 1 (1976-77), pp. 1-10.
Hook, Sidney. Education and the Taming of Power.
    London: Alcove Press, 1974.

Illich, Ivan. De-Schooling Society. New York: Harper &
    Row, 1971.
Joy, Donald, ed. Moral Development Foundations. Nash-
    ville: Abingdon Press, 1983.
Karier, Clarence, Paul Violas, and Joel Spring. Roots of
    Crisis: American Education in the 20th Century.
    Chicago: Rand McNally, 1973.
Katz, Michael. Class, Bureaucracy and Schools. New
    York: Praeger, 1971.
_____. The Irony of Early School Reform. Boston: Beacon
    Press, 1968.
Kazepides, A. C. "The Logic of Values Clarification."
    The Journal of Educational Thought, XI, 2 (August
    1977), pp. 99-111.
Kilpatrick, William, ed. The Teacher and Society. New
    York: Appleton-Century, 1937.
Kirschenbaum, Howard. Advanced Values Clarification. La
    Jolla, Calif.: University Associates, 1977.
_____. "Clarifying Values Clarification: Some Theoretical
    Issues." In Moral Education: It Comes with the
    Territory, D. Purpel and K. Ryan, eds., pp. 116-125.
    Berkeley, Calif.: McCutchan, 1976.
_____. "Recent Research in VC." In Values Education:
    Theory, Practice, Problems, Prospects, J. Meyer, B.
    Burnham, J. Cholvat, eds., pp. 71-78. Waterloo,
    Ontario: Wilfrid Laurier University Press, 1975.
Kirschenbaum, Howard, and Sidney Simon, eds. Readings
    in Values Clarification. Minneapolis: Winston Press,
    1973.
Kniker, Charles. You and Values Education. Columbus,
    Ohio: Charles E. Merrill, 1977.
Kohl, Herbert. 36 Children. London: Victor Gollancz,
    1968.
Kohlberg, Lawrence. "The Child as Moral Philosopher."
    Psychology Today (September 1968), pp. 25-30.
_____. "Cognitive-Developmental Theory and the Practice
    of Collective Moral Education." In Group Care: An
    Israeli Approach: The Educational Path of Youth
    Aliyah, Martin Wolins and Meir Gottesman, eds. New
    York: Gordon and Breach, 1971.
_____, ed. Collected Papers on Moral Development and Moral
    Education. Cambridge, Mass.: Harvard Graduate School
    of Education, 1975.
_____. "Educating for a Just Society: An Updated and Re-
    vised Statement." In Moral Development, Moral Educa-
    tion, and Kohlberg, Brenda Munsey, ed. Birmingham,
    Ala.: Religious Education Press, 1980.
_____. "High School Democracy and Education for a Just
    Society." In Moral Education: A First Generation of
    Research and Development, Ralph Mosher, ed., pp. 20-
    57. New York: Praeger, 1980.
_____. "The Moral Atmosphere of the School." In Read-
    ings in Moral Education, Peter Scharf, ed. Minnea-
    polis: Winston Press, 1978.
_____. "Moral Development and the New Social Studies."
    Social Education, XXXVII, 5 (1973), pp. 369-375.

_____. "Moral Education in the Schools: A Developmental View." School Review, LXXIV, 1 (Spring 1966), pp. 1-29.

_____, ed. The Philosophy of Moral Development. San Francisco: Harper & Row, 1981.

_____, ed. The Psychology of Moral Development. San Francisco: Harper & Row, 1983.

_____. "The Relationship of Moral Education to the Broader Field of Value Education." In Values Education: Theories, Practice, Problems, Prospects, J. Meyer, B. Burnham, J. Cholvat, eds. Waterloo, Ontario: Wilfrid Laurier University Press, 1975.

_____. "A Reply to Owen Flanegan and Some Comments on the Puka-Goodpaster Exchange." Ethics, XCII, 3 (April 1982), pp. 513-528.

_____. "Revisions in the Theory and Practice of Moral Development." In New Directions for Child Development: Moral Education, No. 2, William Damon, ed., pp. 83-88. San Francisco: Jossey-Bass, 1978.

_____. "Stages of Moral Development as a Basis for Moral Education." In Moral Education: Interdisciplinary Approaches, C. M. Beck, B. S. Crittendon, E. V. Sullivan, eds. Toronto: University of Toronto Press, 1971.

_____. "Symposium on Moral Development." Ethics, XCI, 3 (April 1982).

Kohlberg, Lawrence, Kelsey Kauffman, Peter Scharf, and Joseph Hickey. "The Just Community Approach to Corrections: A Theory." Journal of Moral Education, IV, 3 (1975), pp. 243-260.

Kohlberg, Lawrence, and Elliot Turiel. "Moral Development and Moral Education." In Psychology and Educational Practice, Gerald Lesser, ed., pp. 410-465. Glenview, Ill.: Scott, Foresman, 1971.

Kozol, Jonathan. Death at an Early Age. New York: Bantam Books, 1967.

Kuhmerker, L., M. Mentkowski, and V. Erickson. Evaluating Moral Development. Schenectady, N.Y.: Character Research Press, 1980.

Leonard, George. Education and Ecstasy. New York: Delta Books, 1968.

Lickona, Thomas, ed. Moral Development and Behavior. New York: Holt, Rinehart and Winston, 1976.

Lickona, Thomas, et al. A Strategy for Teaching Values. New York: Guidance Associates, 1972.

Lockwood, Alan. "A Critical View of Values Clarification." Teachers College Record, LXXVII, 1 (September 1975), pp. 35-50.

Lukes, Steven. Emile Durkheim, His Life and Work: A Historical and Critical Study. New York: Penguin Books, 1973.

Mapel, Brenda Munsey. "An Act-Theory Alternative to Rationalistic Moral Education." In Philosophy of Education, 1978, Gary Fenstermacher, ed., pp. 85-104. Champaign, Ill.: Philosophy of Education Society, 1979.

Martin, Jane Roland. "Excluding Women from the Educa-
    tional Realm." Harvard Education Review, LII, 2
    (May 1983), pp. 133-148.
_____. "The Ideal of the Educated Person." Educational
    Theory, XXXI, 2 (Spring 1981), pp. 97-109.
_____. "Sophie and Emile: A Case Study of Sex Bias in
    the History of Educational Thought." Harvard Educa-
    tional Review, LI, 3 (August 1981), pp. 357-373.
Matthews, Gareth. Philosophy and the Young Child.
    Cambridge, Mass.: Harvard University Press, 1980.
Maximoff, G. P. The Political Philosophy of Bakunin.
    New York: Free Press, 1953.
May, Philip. Moral Education in School. London: Methuen
    Educational, 1971.
Meyer, John, ed. Reflections on Values Education. Water-
    loo, Ontario: Wilfrid Laurier University Press, 1976.
Miel, Alice. The Short-Changed Children of Suburbia.
    New York: Institute of Human Relations Press, 1967.
Mischel, Theodore, ed. Cognitive Development and Epis-
    temology. New York: Academic Press, 1971.
Moore, Willis. "Indoctrination as a Normative Conception."
    Studies in Philosophy and Education, IV, 4 (Summer
    1966), pp. 396-403.
Mosher, Ralph, ed. Moral Education: A First Generation
    of Research and Development. New York: Praeger,
    1980.
Munsey, Brenda, ed. Moral Development, Moral Education,
    and Kohlberg. Birmingham, Ala.: Religious Education
    Press, 1980.
Musgrave, P. W. The Moral Curriculum: A Sociological
    Analysis. London: Methuen, 1978.
Neil, A. S. The Problem Child. New York: Robert McBride,
    1927.
Nevin, Hugh. "Values Clarification: Perspectives on John
    Dewey with Implications for Religious Education."
    Religious Education, LXXXIII, 6 (November-December
    1978), pp. 661-677.
Niblett, W. R., ed. Moral Education in a Changing
    Society. London: Faber and Faber, 1963.
Nisbet, Robert. The Sociology of Emile Durkheim. New
    York: Oxford University Press, 1974.
Nozick, Robert. Philosophical Explanations. Cambridge,
    Mass.: Harvard University Press, 1981.
Nyberg, David, ed. The Philosophy of Open Education.
    London: Routledge and Kegan Paul, 1971.
Oldenquist, Andrew. "Moral Education Without Moral
    Education: Review Essay." Harvard Educational Re-
    view, XLIX, 2 (May 1979), pp. 240-247.
Ottoway, A. K. C. "The Educational Sociology of Emile
    Durkheim." British Journal of Sociology, VI (1955),
    pp. 213-217.
Parsons, Talcott. "The School as a Social System: Some
    of Its Functions in American Society." Harvard Educa-
    tional Review, XXIX, 4 (1959), pp. 297-318.
_____. The Structure of Social Action. Glencoe, Ill.:
    Free Press, 1949.

Paterson, R. W. K. The Nihilist Egoist: Max Stirner.
    London: Oxford University Press, 1971.
Peters, R. S. Ethics and Education. London: Allen and
    Unwin, 1961.
_____. "General Editor's Note." In Educational Judgment,
    James F. Doyle, ed. London: Routledge and Kegan Paul,
    International Library of the Philosophy of Education,
    1973.
_____, ed. John Dewey Reconsidered. London: Routledge
    and Kegan Paul, 1977.
_____. Moral Development and Moral Education. London:
    George Allen and Unwin, 1981.
Peterson, Howard. "The Quest for Moral Order: Emile
    Durkheim on Education." Journal of Moral Education,
    IV, 1 (October 1974), pp. 39-46.
Porter, Nancy, and Nancy Taylor. How To Assess the
    Moral Reasoning of Students. Toronto: Ontario
    Institute for Studies in Education, 1972.
Postman, Neil, and Charles Weingartner. Teaching as a
    Subversive Activity. New York: Delacorte, 1969.
Power, Clark, and Joseph Reimer. "Moral Atmosphere:
    An Educational Bridge Between Moral Judgment and
    Action." In New Directions for Child Development:
    Moral Development, No. 2, William Damon, ed., pp. 105-
    116. San Francisco: Jossey-Bass, 1978.
Prakash, Madhu Suri. "Moral Education and the Initiation
    Into the Institution of Morality." Philosophy of Edu-
    cation, 1981, Daniel R. De Nicola, ed., pp. 105-114.
    Normal, Ill.: Philosophy of Education Society, 1982.
Puka, Bill. "An Interdisciplinary Treatment of Kohlberg."
    Ethics, XCII, 3 (April 1982), pp. 408-470.
Purpel, D., and K. Ryan, eds. Moral Education: It Comes
    with the Territory. Berkeley, Calif.: McCutchan,
    1976.
Raths, Louis, Merrill Harmin, and Sidney Simon. Values
    and Teaching. Columbus, Ohio: Charles E. Merrill,
    1966.
_____. Values and Teaching. 2d ed. Columbus, Ohio:
    Charles E. Merrill, 1978.
Ratner, Joseph, ed. Intelligence in the Modern World:
    John Dewey's Philosophy. New York: Modern Library,
    1939.
Ravitch, Diane. The Revisionists Revised: A Critique of
    the Radical Attack on the Schools. New York: Basic
    Books, 1978.
Reimer, Everett. School Is Dead: Alternatives in Educa-
    tion. New York: Doubleday, 1971.
Rokeach, Milton. "Towards a Philosophy of Values Educa-
    tion." In Values Education: Theory, Practice, Prob-
    lems, Prospects, J. Meyer, B. Burnham, and J. Cholvat,
    eds. Waterloo, Ontario: Wilfrid Laurier University
    Press, 1975.
_____. Understanding Human Values: Individual and Societal.
    New York: Free Press, 1979.
Rorvick, H. "Content and Form in Kohlberg's Theory of
    Moral Development." Scandinavian Journal of Educa-

tional Research, XXIV, 3 (1980), pp. 105-119.
Rosenzweig, Linda. "Kohlberg in the Classroom: Moral
     Education Models." In Moral Development, Moral Edu-
     cation, and Kohlberg, Brenda Munsey, ed. Birmingham,
     Ala.: Religious Education Press, pp. 359-380.
Saltzstein, Herbert. "Critical Issues in Kohlberg's
     Theory of Moral Reasoning." In Monographs of the
     Society for Research in Child Development, XLVIII,
     1-2 (1983), pp. 108-119.
Scheffler, Israel. Four Pragmatists. London: Routledge
     and Kegan Paul, 1974.
Schilpp, Paul Arthur, ed. The Philosophy of John Dewey.
     La Salle, Ill.: Open Court, 1939.
Schwab, J. J. "The Impossible Role of the Teacher in
     Progressive Education." In Science, Curriculum, and
     Liberal Education: Selected Essays of Joseph J. Schwab,
     Ian Westbury and Neil Wilcox, eds., pp. 167-183.
     Chicago: University of Chicago Press, 1978.
Selman, Robert. "Social-Cognitive Understanding: A Guide
     to Educational and Clinical Practice." In Moral
     Development and Behavior, T. Lickona, ed., pp. 299-
     316. New York: Holt, Rinehart and Winston, 1976.
Simon, Brian, ed. The Radical Tradition in Education in
     Britain. London: Lawrence and Wishart, 1972.
Simon, Sidney. "A Reply to Stewart." Phi Delta Kappan,
     LVI, 10 (June 1975).
_____. "Values Clarification vs. Indoctrination." Social
     Education (December 1971), pp. 902-905.
Simon, Sidney, and Polly de Sherbinin. "Values Clarifi-
     cation: It Can Start Gently and Grow Deep." Phi Delta
     Kappan, LVI, 10 (June 1975), pp. 679-683.
Simon, Sidney, Leland Howe, and Howard Kirschenbaum.
     Values Clarification. New York: Hart, 1972.
Simon, Sidney, and Lawrence Kohlberg. "An Exchange of
     Opinion Between Kohlberg and Simon." Learning
     (December 1972).
Simon, Sidney, and Sally Wendkos Olds. Helping Your Child
     Learn Right from Wrong: A Guide to Values Clarifi-
     cation. New York: Simon and Schuster, 1976.
Simon, Sidney, and P. O'Rourke. Developing Values with
     Exceptional Children. Englewood Cliffs, N.J.:
     Prentice-Hall, 1977.
Singer, Marcus. Generalization in Ethics. New York:
     Knopf, 1961.
Sizer, Nancy, and Theodore Sizer, eds. Moral Education:
     Five Lectures. Cambridge, Mass.: Harvard University
     Press, 1970.
Snook, I. A. Indoctrination and Education. London:
     Routledge and Kegan Paul, 1972.
_____, ed. Concepts of Indoctrination. London: Routledge
     and Kegan Paul, 1972.
Spring, Joel. American Education: An Introduction to
     Social and Political Aspects. New York: Longman,
     1978.
_____. Educating the Worker-Citizen: The Social, Economic

and Political Foundations of Education. New York: Longman, 1980.

_____. Education and the Rise of the Corporate State. Boston: Beacon Press, 1972.

_____. A Primer of Libertarian Education. Montreal: Black Rose Books, 1975.

Stafford, J. Martin. "John Wilson, Prophet of the Sane Society." Journal of Philosophy of Education, XXIII (1979), pp. 167-186.

Stevenson, Leslie. Seven Theories of Human Nature. New York: Oxford University Press, 1974.

Stewart, John. "Problems and Contradictions of Values Clarification." Phi Delta Kappan, LVI, 10 (June 1975), pp. 684-689.

Stirner, Max. The Ego and His Own. New York: Libertarian Book Club, 1963.

_____. The False Principle of Our Education. Colorado Springs, Colo.: Ralph Myles, 1967.

Sullivan, Edmund. Kohlberg's Structuralism, Monograph Series 115. Toronto: Ontario Institute for Studies in Education, 1977.

Sullivan, William. Reconstructing Public Philosophy. Berkeley, Calif.: University of California Press, 1983.

Superka, Douglas. "A Typology of Valuing Theories and Values Education Approaches." Ph.D. diss., School of Education, University of California, Berkeley, 1973.

Superka, Douglas, Christine Ahrens, Judith Hedstrom, Luther Ford, and Patricia Johnson, eds. Values Education Sourcebook: Conceptual Approaches, Materials Analyses, and an Annotated Bibliography. Boulder, Colo.: Social Science Education Consortium, 1976.

Taylor, Monica, ed. Progress and Problems in Moral Education. Windsor, Eng.: NFER Publishing, 1975.

Tolstoi, Lev. Tolstoy on Education. Chicago: University of Chicago Press, 1967.

Toulmin, Stephen. An Examination of the Place of Reason in Ethics. Cambridge: Cambridge University Press, 1960.

Traugott, Mark, ed. Emile Durkheim on Institutional Analysis. Chicago: University of Chicago Press, 1978.

Volkmor, Cora, Anne Pasanella, and Louis Raths. Values in the Classroom. Columbus, Ohio: Charles E. Merrill, 1977.

Wallwork, Ernest. Durkheim: Morality and Milieu. Cambridge, Mass.: Harvard University Press, 1972.

Warnock, G. J. The Object of Morality. London: Methuen, 1971.

Warnock, Mary. Education: A Way Ahead. Oxford: Basil Blackwell, 1979.

_____. Ethics Since 1900. London: Oxford University Press, 1960.

_____. Schools of Thought. London: Faber and Faber, 1977.

Wasserman, Elsa. "An Alternative High School Based on Kohlberg's Just Community Approach to Education."

In <u>Moral Education: A First Generation of Research
and Development</u>, Ralph Mosher, ed., pp. 265-278.
New York: Praeger, 1981.
Watt, A. J. <u>Rational Moral Education</u>. Melbourne:
Melbourne University Press, 1976.
Westbury, Ian, and Neil Wilcox, eds. <u>Science, Curriculum,
and Liberal Education: Selected Essays of Joseph J.
Schwab</u>. Chicago: University of Chicago Press, 1978.
Wilson, John. <u>The Assessment of Morality</u>. Windsor, Eng.:
NFER-NELSON Publishing, 1973.
_____. <u>Education and the Concept of Mental Health</u>.
London: Routledge and Kegan Paul, 1968.
_____. <u>Education in Religion and the Emotions</u>. London:
Heinemann Educational, 1971.
_____. <u>Equality</u>. London: Hutchinson, 1966.
_____. <u>Fantasy and Common Sense in Education</u>. New York:
John Wiley, 1979.
_____. <u>Logic and Sexual Morality</u>. Harmondsworth., Eng.:
Pelican, 1965.
_____. "Moral Education: Retrospect and Prospect."
<u>Journal of Moral Education</u>, IX (October 1979), pp. 3-9.
_____. "Moral Education and the Curriculum." In <u>Progress
and Problems in Moral Education</u>, Monica Taylor, ed.
Windsor, Eng.: NFER-NELSON Publishing, 1975.
_____. <u>Moral Education and the Curriculum</u>. Oxford:
Pergamon, 1969.
_____. <u>Moral Thinking</u>. London: Heinemann Educational,
1970.
_____. <u>Philosophy and Practical Education</u>. London:
Routledge and Kegan Paul, 1977.
_____. <u>Practical Methods of Moral Education</u>. London:
Heinemann Educational, 1972.
_____. <u>Preface to the Philosophy of Education</u>. London:
Routledge and Kegan Paul, 1979.
_____. <u>Reason and Morals</u>. Cambridge: Cambridge University
Press, 1961.
_____. "Reply to J. Martin Stafford." <u>Journal of Philo-
sophy of Education</u>, XXIII (1979), pp. 187-188.
_____. "Teaching and Neutrality." In <u>Progress and Prob-
lems in Moral Education</u>, Monica Taylor, ed., pp. 113-
122. Windsor, Eng.: NFER-NELSON Publishing, 1977.
Wilson, John, Norman Williams, and Barry Sugarman.
<u>Introduction to Moral Education</u>. Harmondsworth,
Eng.: Penguin, 1967.
Wolff, Kurt, ed. <u>Emile Durkheim</u>. Columbus: Ohio State
University Press, 1960.
Wolins, Martin, and Meir Gottesman, eds., <u>Group Care: An
Israeli Approach: The Educational Path of Youth Aliyah</u>.
New York: Gordon and Breach, 1971.

INDEX

Action, moral: concept of, 4-5; Dewey on, 110-111; Durkheim on, 20-21, 110-111; Kohlberg on, 81-83, 110; values clarification and, 57-59, 110; Wilson on, 38, 110

Addams, Jane, 97

Aesthetics, 23; Durkheim on, 17

Affect. *See* Feelings

Anti-moral-education movement: described, 91-93; empirical evaluative argument in, 98-99; epistemological argument in, 93-95; individualist argument in, 95-97, 103; socialist argument in, 97-98; structural argument in, 99-100; tradition of, 100-102

Aristotle, 81, 82

Authority of teachers, 24, 27

Autonomy: anti-moral-education movement and, 95-98; Durkheim on, 17, 21, 27; Wilson on, 30-31, 35. *See also* Social/individual nature of morality

Averich, Paul, 91-92

Bakunin, Mikhail Aleksandrovich, 96-97

Bereiter, Carl, 93, 94, 99, 100, 101

"Beyond Values Clarification" (Kirschenbaum), 45

Blasi, Augusto, 82

Blatt, Moshe, 88

Bowles, Samuel, 97

Calvert, Bruce, 94, 101, 109, 113-114

Carnegie-Mellon Education project, 88-89

Choosing in values clarification, 48, 52, 53, 56, 58, 59

Civilization and Its Discontents (Freud), 11

"Clarifying Values Clarification: Some Theoretical Issues" (Kirschenbaum), 45

Coleman and Jencks (studies), 98

Communicating in values clarification, 48, 56

Content/form of morality: concept of, 3-4; Dewey on, 109-110; Durkheim on, 19-20, 109-110; Kohlberg on, 80-81, 109; values clarification and, 55-56, 109; Wilson on, 37-38, 109

Creativity from social interaction, 11

Deeds. *See* Action, moral

"Determination of Moral Facts" (Durkheim), 12

"Development as the Aim of Education" (Kohlberg), 70

Dewey, John, 47, 54, 67, 69, 70, 83, 97, 101; on content/form of morality, 109-110; on indoctrination, 113-115; on moral action, 110-111; John Dewey Society, 116; on the morally educated person, 111-113; moral principles of, 107; on pedagogy, 117-118; on reason in ethics, 107-109; on social/individual nature of morality, 104-105; on teachers, 116-117

Discipline, Durkheim on, 17, 19, 21

"Discussion of the Effectiveness of Moral Doctrines" (Durkheim), 17, 18